In an eye-opening passage at the beginning of *Reviving Your First Love*, the author confides:

"And what of my love for the Lord? I was familiar with the passage in Revelation in which Jesus said to the church at Ephesus: 'I have this against you, that you have left your first love.' My own love for Jesus, while once fervent, had dimmed and I hardly knew how to revive it."

In the midst of life's entanglements, Rena Newton's spiritual hunger prevailed and led her to God's Word, and repentance, out of which she found her love for Jesus deepened and revitalized.

Now, for all who want to deepen their own love for the Lord, *Reviving Your First Love* identifies three fundamental steps:

- *Confessing sin and God's remedy*
- *Making a covenant with the Lord*
- *Writing a prayer of agreement*

Rena Newton discovered the reality of God's gift of repentance through prayer. *Reviving Your First Love* is her gift to you.

Reviving Your First Love

RENA NEWTON

Published by
√ chosen books

FLEMING H. REVELL COMPANY
OLD TAPPAN, NEW JERSEY

Scripture references are taken from the New American Standard Bible, copyright © The Lockman Foundation 1960, 1962, 1963, 1968, 1971, 1972, 1973, 1975, 1977.

Scripture references marked KJV are taken from the King James Version of the Bible.

Italics are added by the author.

Library of Congress Cataloging in Publication Data

Newton, Rena.
    Reviving your first love / Rena Newton.
        p.   cm.
    "A Chosen book"—T.p. verso.
    ISBN 0-8007-9139-8
    1. Spiritual life. I. Title.
BV4501.2.N54   1989
248.4—dc19   88-13780
                                                                  CIP

A Chosen Book
Copyright 1989 by Rena Newton
Chosen Books are published by
Fleming H. Revell Company
Old Tappan, New Jersey
Printed in the United States of America

Dedication

*T*his book is dedicated to my husband, Phil, who loved and cherished me when my ground was most fallow, and to our three precious children, Philip, Mark, and Rena Carolyn, who have been a source of joy, inspiration, and encouragement to me.

Acknowledgments

Special thanks to those who helped with the typing and proofreading: Rhonda Arnold, Roberta Stoner, Tina Fiol, DeWanna Higdon, and Rena Carolyn Newton. Thanks, too, to Glenda Sholl, Germaine Copeland, Margaret Welsh, Eve Roebuck, Sherry Hufham and her late mother, Mary Russell, Janice Blalock, Joy Martin, Annette Walls, Fran Ewing, Quin Sherrer, and a host of others whose lives influenced profoundly the writing of the manuscript. Last but not least, I owe a debt of gratitude to Len LeSourd and Jane Campbell for their editorial skills and patience that helped bring this work to completion.

Contents

IV. ON TO HIGHER GROUND

Foreword

A few years ago my wife, Rena, began a quest for more of Christ in her life. Something was missing in her faith that was there earlier in her Christian walk. The probing she did and the results of this quest are revealed in this book, *Reviving Your First Love.*

In every believer's life it is necessary to break up the hard ground before the Spirit of God can produce fruit. This book gives practical ways to deal with these fleshly hindrances in order that one may experience the fullness of a transformed life. The principles Rena applies in these pages are timeless because of the need for total dependence on God's eternal, infallible, and inerrant Word.

The multitudes of believers and unbelievers who desire a release from the bondages that ensnare them need to know that *Reviving Your First Love* not only opens a way to be freed of these entanglements, but provides practical training in the use of the Bible—the sword of the Spirit—to cut away all such bondage.

I am blessed to share in this book not only as a reader but as an intimate spectator. I have seen firsthand God's marvelous work in Rena's life. Her life has truly been transformed by the methods shown in the book. Part of my joy has been to watch this metamorphosis take place. The newness and the freshness have produced a fragrant aroma of the Lord's life that our family and friends continue to enjoy.

This book has been a guideline to all the members of our family; in fact, it has changed our lives. We trust that all who read it will not only find it a faith-strengthener, but will also come to know Jesus as Lord of all.

Philip T. Newton, Jr., M.D.

Guidelines
for the Reader

My guess is that you picked up this book out of curiosity—and perhaps with a spiritual hunger that has been with you for some time. I wrote it out of a deep hunger to know more of God, to overcome besetting sins in my life, and to return to Jesus as my first love.

It has happened to me! It can happen to you!

I suggest you use *Reviving Your First Love* as a handbook. Decide that you are going to take a journey. Put any label on it that would meet your deepest spiritual need, such as:

My Search for Holiness
A New Beginning with the Lord
Learning to Love God in a New Way
My Quest for Righteousness

Set up a time frame for the above. A month. Three months. Six months. Don't put any time pressure on yourself. I spent most of a year in my journey.

Next, find time *each day* to do it. If you are an early riser, take an hour before breakfast to read a section of this book, praying as you do that the Lord will speak to you about your own failures, weaknesses, sins of omission and commission. Look up all the Scriptures, write down those you want to memorize.

Then use the section "Meditation Response" to do a kind of self-inventory, much as I have done. Answer the questions. Be tough on yourself. You can't lie to God; He reads your heart.

Finally, ask the Lord for His Word to *you*. You may not hear His voice right away. It may not come when you want it to; it happens at His timing, not yours. You probably won't hear an audible voice; more often it's a whisper or a thought in your mind. Most of the time you will get real help and guidance from Him by meditating on His Word. That's why I've included so many Scriptures. I suggest that you also ask God to bring to your remembrance the Scriptures He wants you to have.

As you go along on this journey, use the "Meditation Response" section, in conjunction with a separate notebook, to record the things that happen to you which you see as the fruit of your time with Him. List any failures or unpleasant experiences, and see what God might be teaching you through them.

Let me also suggest that you ask the Lord to lead you to a prayer partner—perhaps your spouse, perhaps a good friend—for mutual support in your spiritual journeys. This is a tremendous encouragement, since two people are seldom "down" at the same time: "If either of them falls, the one will lift up his companion" (Ecclesiastes 4:10). In addition, there is spiritual power in agreement: "If two of you agree on earth about anything that they may ask, it shall be done for them by My Father who is in heaven" (Matthew 18:19).

I pray that you decide to embark on this adventure. It began a process inside me to make me less self-centered; it enlarged my vision and brought me closer to God. In fact, it opened the door to a dynamic new life!

May the Lord bless you in a very special way.

Rena Newton

PART I

A
JOURNEY
BEGUN

The Missing Ingredient

Clearing the breakfast dishes after kissing the children and sending them out to wait for the carpool driver several years ago, I was thinking how good it would be to crawl back into bed for another hour of sleep.

The shrill ring of the telephone interrupted my thoughts.

"Rena, can you take the kids to school? My car won't start."

Oh no, I groaned inwardly, knowing we were already in trouble with the school due to the tardiness of the other two drivers. I snapped, "Couldn't you have called earlier?" Irritation rose up in me and began to boil over as I thought how my children would be penalized for being late—and it would be the other mother's fault, not their own.

"O.K., give me a minute, I'll pick them all up," I said, noticing my hand shaking as I put down the receiver. Grabbing my keys, I thought back to the day we'd tried to organize this carpool. We were all Christians, yet nothing about our organizational meeting sounded very Christian. Each of us had our own little individual schedule preferences.

Now when my friend, my sister in Christ, needed my support when she had car trouble, I had snapped at her.

"O God, I can't cope with even the small annoyances in my life anymore," I breathed as I backed the car out of the driveway.

I hardly noticed the children's chatter as I made a quick review of my situation, driving them to school.

If Phil ever came in and found me sleeping late, he'd say, "Honey, I know you need more sleep than other people. So get your rest."

But I knew it wasn't all right. I was becoming addicted to sleep, though I'd always rationalize that I did need more sleep.

Could I ever stop being a slave to sleep? Or getting angry with my Christian friend when her car stalled and I was inconvenienced by having to drive the children to school myself? Or being impatient when those I loved failed to live up to my expectations? Or getting frustrated when things didn't go smoothly?

I was acquainted with enough Scripture to guess that the blockage in my life was called "sin" in the Bible. But I had been a Christian for years. Surely there must be some way of escape from such selfishness.

Where was the joy in my life? I had once tasted it fully, but lately it seemed transient and elusive. What a contrast to the consistent, overflowing, effervescent joy promised in the Scripture.[1] Was there a way to maintain joy?

And what of my love for the Lord? I was familiar with the passage in the book of Revelation in which Jesus said to the church at Ephesus: "I have this against you, that you have left your first love."[2] My own love for Jesus, while once fervent, had dimmed, and I hardly knew how to revive it.

The answer to this problem came to me through the pages of a book entitled *True and False Repentance* by Charles Finney. This book totally changed my life! Though it was written well over a hundred years ago, its ink seemed scarcely dry on the pages. Its message for me was like a disc plowing up fallow ground.

For years my life had been an enigma. Outwardly I had grown up with everything that should have made me happy: loving parents, friends, popularity and honors beyond any of my expectations. Even in my adult life blessings abounded: I loved my nursing profession, and I later met and married a wonderful man who cherished me and provided abundantly for all my material needs. The Lord had even given us three precious, healthy children. What more could anyone ask?

Even though I was already a Christian who years before had experienced a mighty touch of God's power, today I wasn't truly fulfilled. Something was missing. Unfortunately, the very blessings that should have wrought gratitude and humility in me had instead left me spoiled and self-centered. Frustration and guilt inevitably followed. I was disgusted with myself, and regrettably I often took it out on those I loved the most.

One particular episode stands out in my mind: Phil had made a decision that took our family in a direction different from what I felt strongly was God's will. Ordinarily Phil and I had an unusually good relationship, but I believe God brought about this whole set of circumstances to deal with rebellion in me. I struggled for months with anger and bitterness toward Phil over this decision. I sought repeatedly to let go of the resentment, but it clung to me as though it had tentacles. As the cancer of unforgiveness grew, I realized the problem was more mine than Phil's.

One day after a heated argument over the subject, I stormed furiously to our bedroom. Hysterical and miserable, I screamed out to the Lord, "Please, *don't leave me this way!*"

I'm amazed that God would speak to me at all while I was in such a state, but very quietly in my spirit I heard,

Romans 8:28. I knew it by heart: "And we know that God causes all things to work together for good to those who love God, to those who are called according to His purpose."

"What in the world does *that* Scripture have to do with my present predicament?" I questioned. "All things, yes, except sin. How could Romans 8:28 apply to the resentment I've felt toward Phil?"

Then I felt the Lord say, *He who is forgiven much, loves much.*[3]

Perplexed, I sought to understand what God was trying to show me. Certainly He hadn't issued a *carte blanche* permission slip for sinning, that I might love Him more. "God forbid!" as the apostle Paul would say. God knew how I longed to be set free from this bondage. Then revelation came.

"Lord, are You saying You are going to work all things together for good by causing me to hate all sin in my life and then to love You in proportion to all the sin for which You have forgiven me?" I couldn't imagine *that* degree of love! But I received that word as a promise then and there and held onto it for years, though at times the fulfillment of it seemed a million miles away.

Reconciliation with Phil finally came, but I continued to flounder and vacillate from defeat to short-lived victory. Often my aspirations unto godliness faded into ineffective attempts to cope with the pressures of everyday living. My level of frustration mounted when I read in the Bible about the abundant life Jesus promised those who receive Him[4] and about "the exceeding greatness of His power toward us who believe."[5] I *had* received Jesus[6] and I *did* believe He was the Son of God,[7] yet why was I not able to tap into that power? For the most part, my life seemed a far cry from the apostle Paul's bold declaration, "If any man is in Christ, he is a new creature; the old things passed away; behold, new things have come" (2 Corinthians 5:17). What was my problem? Certainly there must be a reason for the block of sin preventing me from experiencing this new and abundant life.

The impact of Charles Finney's book *True and False Repentance* intensified as the words I had heard years earlier from the lips of Catherine Marshall reverberated in my thoughts: "The Lord has shown me clearly that whenever I fall flat on my face over and over again in the same areas, it is because I have not truly repented."

As I read *True and False Repentance*, I was astounded by the realization that I had deceived myself regarding the whole matter of repentance. I learned that most of what I had experienced came clearly under the heading of "false repentance," which springs from "worldly sorrow." This worldly sorrow may cause great regret for the consequences of sin or the uneasy guilt it produces, but it is totally void of any true abhorrence of sin *solely* because this sin grieves the heart of God. I saw that false repentance is rooted inevitably in selfishness.

From Finney's book, I understood why he was considered by many to be the greatest revivalist the world has ever known. He wrote with authority, out of his own experience, and zeroed in on motives of the heart. He also described true repentance—deep, thorough, permanent. I was forced to admit I knew nothing of it. Finney was convinced the lack of true repentance was the main reason for "the present deplorable state of the Church."

I became convinced my lack of true repentance was the main reason for the present deplorable state of my own Christian life. And this only backed up the further admonition of Jesus to the church at Ephesus that had left its first love. "Remember therefore from where you have fallen," He said, "and repent and do the deeds you did at first; or else I am coming to you, and will remove your lampstand out of its place—unless you repent."[8]

Through Catherine Marshall's statement, the Lord had

gently but firmly planted a seed in my heart regarding the meaning of repentance. Now, through Finney's book, that seed was beginning to take root. But the harvest was yet to come!

Although *True and False Repentance* enlightened me as to what biblical repentance was—the kind John the Baptist spoke of when he thundered, "Bring forth fruit in keeping with repentance"—I still wasn't sure how to go about obtaining it.

I turned to the Bible for the answer. Through Scripture, I saw that repentance was not something I could work up or generate in my own strength but, as in all aspects of salvation, was a gift from God:

> "[Jesus Christ] is the one whom God exalted to His right hand as a Prince and a Savior, to grant repentance to Israel, and forgiveness of sins."
>
>   Acts 5:31

> "Well then, God has granted to the Gentiles also the repentance that leads to life."
>
>   Acts 11:18b

> And the Lord's bond-servant must not be quarrelsome, but be kind to all, able to teach, patient when wronged, with gentleness correcting those who are in opposition, if perhaps God may grant them repentance leading to the knowledge of the truth.
>
>   2 Timothy 2:24–25

> For the sorrow that is according to the will of God produces a repentance without regret, leading to salvation; but the sorrow of the world produces death.
>
>   2 Corinthians 7:10

I grieved to think how often I had ignored or even refused God's bountiful gifts. They were there for the receiving, yet I knew He respected my free will and would never force any of His gifts on me. How deadly the effect of apathy! It was to those who diligently seek Him that He promised the reward (Hebrews 11:6).

Realizing repentance was a gift from God, I determined to seek Him for it, confident He would not withhold from me what was clearly His will (2 Peter 3:9). I might have made the mistake of seeking the gift of repentance instead of the Giver, if the Lord had not spoken to me so specifically from Psalm 27:8:

> When Thou didst say, "Seek My face," my heart said to Thee, "Thy face, O Lord, I shall seek."

He showed me that whatever my need, it would be met only in Him and in Him alone; that getting my needs met was but a byproduct of coming to Him.

As I began to seek the Lord, some interesting Scriptures surfaced. One cold, bleak winter morning, which seemed to symbolize my inward spiritual state, these words were illumined to me from Jeremiah:

> Thus says the Lord . . . "Break up your fallow ground, and do not sow among thorns. Circumcise yourselves to the Lord and remove the foreskins of your heart."
>
> Jeremiah 4:3–4

I remembered from the parable of the sower in Mark 4:19 what Jesus had called thorns—"the worries of the world, and the deceitfulness of riches, and the desires for other things." Yes, putting other things before God and His Word had taken its toll in my life. The thorns had to go!

I sensed the anticipation of springtime as a parallel passage from Hosea came alive, further preparing me for the Lord's next instruction:

> Sow with a view to righteousness, reap in accordance with
> kindness; break up your fallow ground, for it is time to
> seek the Lord until He comes to rain righteousness on you.
>
> Hosea 10:12

Here it was again: "Break up your fallow ground." It seemed to be connected with the law of sowing and reaping: "Do not be deceived, God is not mocked; for whatever a man sows, this he will also reap. For the one who sows to his own flesh [self-centered nature] shall from the flesh reap corruption, but the one who sows to the Spirit shall from the Spirit reap eternal life" (Galatians 6:7–8).

What had been the result of sowing to my flesh? Fallow ground! But here also was a glorious promise: If I would break up my fallow ground and seek the Lord, He would come and rain righteousness on me! How I was beginning to hunger and thirst for righteousness. Yes, self-centeredness was the pits. And I was desperate for a way out.

A few days after I got the book on repentance, a friend called saying she had another book by Charles Finney on revival. She knew how excited I was about *True and False Repentance* and wanted to see what I thought of this leatherbound, five-hundred-page volume entitled *Revivals of Religion*. Hungrily thumbing the contents the very next day, I decided to begin with the chapter "How to Promote Revival." I could hardly believe my eyes when I saw the heading of the chapter: *How to break up your fallow ground!* Glory to His name; I knew He was going to do a mighty thing!

Finney defined fallow ground as ground that has once been tilled, but that has been allowed to lay waste, thus becoming hardened, matted down, and unable to receive seed. His premise was that in order to break up this fallow ground, the ground of our hearts, one must review and confess sins very specifically. He listed twenty-seven types of sin, such as lack of love for God, unbelief, pride, hypocrisy, neglect of self-denial, criticalness, neglect of the Bible and prayer, etc.

When I saw that breaking up my fallow ground required confessing sins, my first reaction was, "But I've already done that; I've confessed my sins all my life." Yet I sensed God was after something deeper here. He wanted to break every yoke of bondage. I also knew unmistakably He had led me thus far and the next step was up to me. I decided I couldn't risk disobeying.

Thus began a six- to eight-month exercise before the Lord. In a thorough, ruthless plowing-up, I confessed my sins in detail *as His Spirit convicted me.* I confessed present failings as well as failings of my whole life past. Looking at myself and my sinfulness before this time had only gotten me deeper into the pit. I had quite a propensity to condemn myself. But this time God's Spirit led me to Scripture after Scripture showing me what *He* had to say about each of these sins *and the way to come out of them.*

I was discovering in a new way the power of the Word of God! For the first time in my life I was agreeing with what God had to say about me, instead of what I felt about myself. I found myself confessing not only my wretchedness apart from Him, but what I was and could be *in Him.*

God said that I am accepted in the Beloved (Ephesians 1:6).

He said that I am more than a conqueror and an overcomer (Romans 8:37).

He said that if I walk in the light, the blood of Jesus cleanses *all* my sin (1 John 1:7).

He said that I am the righteousness of God in Jesus Christ (2 Corinthians 5:21).

Instead of getting further bogged down in the mire, I was getting more and more edified and filled with hope. Faith was being conceived that God could produce godliness even in me! Little did I know the radical transformation of my life that was to be the fruit of my adventure.

For years I had labored to overcome sin, falsely assuming, as Hudson Taylor once did, that practical holiness was to be attained gradually by the diligent use of the means of grace. I did not realize that even though I said I believed "God is love," my life was evidence that I really believed the lie that God was a hard taskmaster. When I looked at His commandments and what I felt He required of me, I always came up short.

Since childhood, I felt subconsciously that I had to earn God's love. But the harder I tried to be a good girl, a good student, a good wife, a good mother—the more I failed. Fear of rejection left me insecure. As a Christian, I knew intellectually to depend upon the power of the Holy Spirit within me, but to appropriate that power was another matter. I was beginning to think God's standard was just too high to attain. At times I felt like giving up.

I was pierced when I read in the epistle of 1 John, "For this is the love of God, that we keep His commandments; and His commandments are not burdensome" (5:3). Then why were they so hard for me? I longed to have the motive for everything I did be love for Him, instead of fear or duty. I needed a deeper revelation of Jesus as He truly was. I could only conclude I must not really *know* Him after all. Falling for Satan's lie about the character of God—that He was an impossible taskmaster—had resulted in a dreadful snare—unbelief.

Oswald Chambers wrote in *My Utmost for His Highest*, "Unless we can face squarely the blackest, ugliest fact without its doing damage to the character of God, we have not yet come to know Him." And I was convinced the only way I could come to know Him, so nothing that ever happened to me could assault His character, was by being rooted and grounded in His Word.

Forever etched in my memory was a scene from the movie *The Hiding Place*. All around Betsie and Corrie ten Boom in the dreaded German extermination camp,

Ravensbrück, women were railing and complaining, howling insults at God and asking, "Why?" Betsie's sure response: "If you really *know* Him, you don't have to ask why!" She and Corrie knew He was good in spite of all the screaming circumstantial evidence to the contrary. That knowledge had been instilled in them long before as they had come to know His ways.

I thought of how the children of Israel remained stiff-necked, murmuring and complaining about every hardship in the wilderness.[9] Psalm 103:7, I believed, explained the reason: The people of Israel knew His acts, but Moses knew His ways. Only with such knowledge could Moses remain the meekest man on earth.

Knowing Him! This, then, has become my goal. I cannot fully describe the transformation of my life brought about since the breaking up of my fallow ground. Glimpses of it are revealed in the last pages of the handbook that follows. Suffice it to say, God has made me brand-new! My eyes had been dim from looking at other things, but He has anointed my eyes with eyesalve.[10] Now I can better behold Jesus in all His glory. Oh, the beauty of His holiness![11] Truly, in the words of the songwriter, "the things of earth have grown strangely dim." My ears had been dull of hearing, for I had listened to other voices, but He has opened my ears.[12] What a blessing now to hear clearly the voice of my Shepherd.[13]

My heart had been hardened by the accumulation of little disobediences, but He has circumcised my heart[14] with the sword of His Word.[15] What joy now to obey Him out of a heart of love.[16] I am continually awed by such a visible manifestation of the grace of God! And I believe it was only through this plowing up that He has removed the scales from my eyes and has begun to grant me a spirit of wisdom and revelation in the knowledge of Jesus (Ephesians 1:17). What rest, liberty, love, and abundant life flourish in this reviving of my first love.[17] In His presence, as David wrote, is fullness of joy (Psalm 16:11).

One of the firstfruits of having mounds of clutter cleared away from my life was a far greater awareness of and concern for the needs of others. A new spiritual sensitivity enabled me to perceive the heart cry of hurting people. It seemed to me that many others were crying out in various ways to be set free, just as I had been.

I sensed that God, by a sovereign act of grace, was causing a move of His people on the earth today. A people hungry for truth, who are sick and tired of bondage, hypocrisy, and a watered-down gospel. A people willing to take off the masks and pay whatever price is necessary to bring the Kingdom of God on earth—the Kingdom that the Bible says "is not eating and drinking, but righteousness and peace and joy in the Holy Spirit" (Romans 14:17).

Confession of sin is never a pleasant thing to do, nor is it something God wants us to dwell on in an unhealthy, introspective way. But confession and repentance, combined with faith, were established by Jesus as prerequisites for entering His glorious Kingdom of Light.[18]

I do believe that the message of repentance is needed as much today as when Charles Finney delivered it to his generation. I am confident the Lord will manifest Himself exceeding abundantly beyond all we might ask or think[19] to anyone who will obey His Word from the heart. This journal, then, is offered as a handbook or tool in learning how to *revive* our first love.[20]

Before beginning, it may be helpful to identify three areas that were the main contributing factors to the mighty deliverance the Lord has wrought in my life:

1. Confessing Sin and God's Remedy

A sure key to victory over sin is not only confessing our guilt before God, but also agreeing with what His Word says about His provision to deliver us from the power of sin.

When confessing my sin, I chose to use the words of

Scripture to describe myself. If Scripture called a certain act wicked or evil, for example, then I called it that. If it considered something an act of blasphemy, I named it such. If it referred to loving something in my life more than I loved God as idolatry or harlotry, then I used those terms. Though some might be offended by such language, I believe God is satisfied and even pleased as we agree with Him about our sin.

2. Making a Covenant with the Lord

He showed me that this was one of the most necessary parts of repentance—unreserved commitment. Just as commitment is the one thing that holds a marriage together when things get tough, it is also the thing that binds us to the Lord. As a teenager I had received Jesus as my Savior and had always desired for Him to be my Lord, but I had never actually turned my life over to Him with no strings attached. He would not let me rest until this matter was settled.

Finally, trusting Him to keep me faithful, I wrote down my commitment one day, sealing it once and for all. In this covenant *He* is the partner with all the power!

God impressed me months later that I had no idea of the significance of that day. I sensed He was saying: "Though My covenant with you was established before the earth was brought forth, yet I wait and long for the day when My children will trust Me enough to respond to My covenant reciprocally. My power at that point in the lives of My children is unlimited. Truly, not until then am I bound by My covenant faithfulness to unleash My unlimited power on their behalf!"

3. Writing a Prayer of Agreement

There is power in agreement, as we have already noted. As the Scripture says, "If two of you agree on earth about anything that they may ask, it shall be done for them by My Father who is in heaven" (Matthew 18:19).

I used this means of power and agreed with my husband for deliverance from several lifelong habits and besetting sins. And it worked! Hallelujah!

The particular Prayer of Agreement I include in this book (see page 114) was taken partly from Joan Cavanaugh's powerful book *More of Jesus, Less of Me*. Combined with the two previously listed activities—confessing sin by using God's words for it and making a covenant with Him—it was the turning point for me.

Though there are usually no formulas in the spiritual walk, there are certain fundamental steps we must take before entering into God's rest—that wonderful state of ceasing from our own labor and totally trusting Him to do all the work in us.[21] The natural result of truly knowing Him is rest, sweet rest.

It is my prayer that this book will be used in other lives to "encourage [them] day after day, as long as it is still called 'Today,' lest any one of [you] be hardened by the deceitfulness of sin" (Hebrews 3:13).

Jesus will not return to receive a Church that is weak, defeated, and overcome with sin and worldliness. He will return to claim a glorious, spotless, victorious bride,[22] whose lamps overflow with oil,[23] and whose main purpose and passion in life is to do the bidding of her Bridegroom and King. I believe Jesus is waiting for His people to take seriously His command to "break up your fallow ground."[24]

Following are some Scripture guides to help us break up our fallow ground:

> When Thou didst say, "Seek My face," my heart said to Thee, "Thy face, O Lord, I shall seek."
>
> Psalm 27:8

"Return, O faithless sons, I will heal your faithlessness."
"Behold, we come to Thee; for Thou art the Lord our God."

Jeremiah 3:22

"Let us lie down in our shame, and let our humiliation cover us; for we have sinned against the Lord our God, we and our fathers, since our youth even to this day. And we have not obeyed the voice of the Lord our God."

Jeremiah 3:25

"Break up your fallow ground, and do not sow among thorns. Circumcise yourselves to the Lord and remove the foreskins of your heart."

Jeremiah 4:3–4

Sow with a view to righteousness, reap in accordance with kindness; break up your fallow ground, for it is time to seek the Lord until He comes to rain righteousness on you.

Hosea 10:12

My Covenant
with the
Lord

*F*ather, as I begin this journey of faith, I make a confession with my mouth, trusting You to work into my heart the change needed. Unless You do that, Lord, it will be only another shallow intention with no real content or resolution. You are the source of my will;[1] therefore I make a decision this day, by Your keeping power,[2] to commit my life to You without reservation, with no conditions attached. Lord, I give You my life in all the mess it is in. Yes, I covenant with You that I am, as of this day, dead to myself and my old life and alive unto You, the living God, my Savior.

I no longer have any rights, any purpose other than to do Your will. But Your will is good and acceptable and perfect. Your will is for me to be victorious in every area.

Lord, I am so tired of living for myself—truly as I have sown to my flesh, I have reaped corruption and misery.[3] Thank You that only in Your Spirit is there life and peace.[4] I ask You to keep me faithful to this covenant by Your power. Jesus, my High Priest, please take this confession before my Father, and Your Father, and intercede for me that my faith in You will not fail, though Satan would desire to sift me as wheat.[5]

Lord, please change my desires, my heart, my thoughts, as I seek You for the renewal of my mind. Deliver me from the enemy and any spirits that have had me in bondage. I release any and everyone from my judgment. I choose to forgive and accept.

Father, I confess and repent of anxiety about Your ability to sanctify me and even my willingness to allow You to. I place my heart and my will into Your hands and trust You with them. Forgive me for anxiety and lack of trust and cleanse me of this sin. Father, I look to You for the direction of my life and for Your will and power for this day. I praise You for Your faithfulness to me—Your covenant faithfulness.

Scripture Guide

To Thee, O Lord, I lift up my soul. O my God, in Thee I trust, do not let me be ashamed; do not let my enemies [the flesh, the powers of darkness] exult over me."

Psalm 25:1–2

Do not remember the sins of my youth.

Psalm 25:7

Shew me thy ways, O Lord; teach me thy paths.

Psalm 25:4, KJV

Create in me a clean heart, O God, and renew a steadfast spirit within me. . . . Sustain me with a willing spirit.

Psalm 51:10, 12

He that covereth his sins shall not prosper: but whoso confesseth and forsaketh them shall have mercy.

Proverbs 28:13, KJV

PART II

SINS
OF
OMISSION

Lack of Love for God

*F*ather, as I begin this time with You, I confess that I have left my first love and broken the first commandment—to love the Lord my God with all my heart, soul, mind, and strength.[1] I have also had other gods before You,[2] and played the harlot by going after them: self, pleasure, sleep, food, friends, family, ease, and comfort.

I also confess that I have not preferred You over all else, Lord.

I have blasphemed You with my wicked tongue and evil heart.

I have not kept my heart with all diligence toward You.[3]

I have not stayed my mind on You that I might be kept in perfect peace by way of trusting in You.[4]

I have called You a liar by my actions and behavior.

By disobedience, I have shown no fear of You.

For all these sins against You and for offending You, I ask Your forgiveness and cleansing. Father, grant me true godly sorrow that works repentance for this sin.[5] Make it a permanent work that will seal my heart to You in love forever.

I marvel at those scriptural truths about Your love—it is not that I loved You, but that You first loved me;[6] that Your love is shed abroad in my heart by the Holy Spirit.[7] And so my commitment today is this: I *will* love the Lord my God with all my heart. I *will* love the Lord my God with all my soul. I *will* love the Lord my God with all my mind. I *will* love the Lord my God with all my strength.[8] I throw myself on Your mercy and faithfulness, Lord, to perform it.

Father, You are the One who commanded love[9] and You are the One who supplies it. Apart from You I can do nothing,[10] but with Jesus in me, I can do all things.[11] You promise to supply all my needs according to Your riches in glory by Christ Jesus,[12] and Lord, You are rich in love. *You are love.*[13]

Therefore, with respect to the promises of God, I will not waver in unbelief, but will grow strong in faith, giving glory to You. I am fully persuaded that what You have promised, You are also able to perform.[14] Hallelujah! I receive Your love; I commit myself to seek Your face that I might know You, that in knowing You I would grow to love You with all my heart.

Please reveal Yourself to me, Father, and let me know Your ways, Your character, Your heart. Deal with rebellion in me that would prevent that revelation from coming. Father, I want my motive for serving and obeying You to be love for You and not just duty or even fear.

I knock, seek, and ask for a heart full of love for You,[15] for You are altogether lovely.[16] With growing faith I now receive. That I might know the surpassing greatness of Your power toward me because I believe,[17] make this Scripture prayer a reality in my life, Lord:

Scripture Guide

Whom have I in heaven but Thee? And besides Thee, I desire nothing on earth. My flesh and my heart may fail, but God is the strength of my heart and my portion forever.

Psalm 73:25–26

"I call heaven and earth to witness against you today, that I have set before you life and death, the blessing and the curse. So choose life in order that you may live, you and your descendants, by loving the Lord your God, by obeying His voice, and by holding fast to Him."

Deuteronomy 30:19–20a

Meditation Response

Does this confession strike any additional reactions inside me? If so, I'll write them out below. What actions will I take? What specific things have kept me from a fervent, white-hot love for God? Am I serious enough about my relationship with Him to do anything about these hindrances? If not, am I deceiving myself?

Neglect
of the
Bible

*F*ather, how I have failed in this area! You have given me so much light, so much instruction regarding the power in Your Word, the necessity for it, and dangers of neglecting it. Yet I have been so apathetic and lazy about giving myself to it.

Your Word is forever settled in heaven.[1] It is the number-one way of truly coming to know You and Your character. It is the thing that keeps me from deception, when I obey it, yet I've let the cares of the world and trivial, unimportant things squeeze it out of my life.

Your Word is profitable for teaching, instructing, correcting, rebuking, and training in righteousness,[2] yet I have acted, in pride and haughtiness, as if I could do without it. You tell me, "Don't be conformed to this world and squeezed into its mold, but be transformed by the renewing of your mind, so that you might prove what is the good, acceptable, and perfect will of God."[3] Your Word is the chief means by which my mind is renewed, yet I have continued to ignore this means and think like the world.

Your Word says, "Man does not live by bread alone, but by every word that proceeds out of the mouth of God,"[4] yet I have acted as if I could live by bread—physical food—and many of the wrong kinds of that. Your Word says the grass withers and flowers fade, but Your Word will stand forever.[5]

I confess my neglect of Your Word as sin and that I have grieved and quenched Your Spirit within me. Please forgive me. I stand on Your Word now, which says if I confess my sin to You, You are faithful and just to forgive me and cleanse me in this area.[6] By Your strength and by Your power and by Your Spirit, I will overcome this sin. I begin by committing myself to spend at least [specify an amount of time] each day in Your Word. It is God who works in me both to will and to do His good pleasure.[7] Father, lead me each day to where You would have me devote myself in Your Word. Keep me from the temptation to yield to the flesh. I will, by Your Spirit, hearken to Your voice and obey. Help me to not waste time each day. Thank You, my God.

To think, O Lord, that there are those who would give their very lives just to have a copy of Your Word or even a portion of it. To think how casually I have handled it! What a lack of gratitude I have for the preciousness of it, knowing that unless we, Your people, repent, we might not always have Your Word here in America. Help me to treasure it and hide it diligently in my heart.[8] Forgive me for my apathy. Thank You for another chance. Please open my eyes. Wake me morning by morning.[9]

Scripture Guide

"This book of the law shall not depart from your mouth, but you shall meditate on it day and night, so that you may be careful to do according to all that is written in it; for then you will make your way prosperous, and then you will have success."

Joshua 1:8

How blessed is the man who does not walk in the counsel of the wicked, nor stand in the path of sinners, nor sit in the seat of scoffers! *But his delight is in the law of the Lord, and in His law he meditates day and night.* And he will be like a tree firmly planted by streams of water, which yields its fruit in its season, and its leaf does not wither; and in whatever he does, he prospers.

Psalm 1:1–3

The law of the Lord is perfect, converting the soul: the testimony of the Lord is sure, making wise the simple. The statutes of the Lord are right, rejoicing the heart: the commandment of the Lord is pure, enlightening the eyes. The fear of the Lord is clean, enduring for ever: the judgments of the Lord are true and righteous altogether. More to be desired are they than gold, yea, than much fine gold: sweeter also than honey and the honeycomb. Moreover by them is thy servant warned: and in keeping of them there is great reward.

Psalm 19:7–11, KJV

Thy word I have treasured in my heart, that I may not sin against Thee.

Psalm 119:11

[Jesus said to the Pharisees,] "You search the Scriptures, because you think that in them you have eternal life; and it is these that bear witness of Me."

John 5:39

"If you abide in My word, then you are truly disciples of Mine; and you shall know the truth, and the truth shall make you free."

John 8:31–32

"If you abide in Me, and My words abide in you, ask whatever you wish, and it shall be done for you."

John 15:7

Meditation Response

What consequences do I recognize in my life due to my neglect of reading and obeying God's Word? What are some of the things that rob me of time spent in God's Word? How can I begin to reprioritize my life to give the Word its proper place? Is there a friend who might help me in this area? Am I willing to make myself vulnerable and accountable by asking for help?

Unbelief

Lord, You've been dealing with me for years regarding this sin. You have shown me that it is the root of all other sin in my life. You've shown me that the opposite of unbelief—faith—is the key to coming out of all my problems. Father, I confess so much underlying doubt in my heart, seeds of doubt planted by the enemy and fed by the world, to which I have not dealt a death blow. I have actually nurtured them by ruminating on them and by letting my thoughts and mind be controlled more by the enemy than by You.

I have suppressed the truth, Lord, and have often chosen to believe the lies of the enemy rather than Your truth.[1] In so doing I have called You a liar and have not even sought You to deliver me from this pattern of thinking. I have not been careful to take thoughts captive, when they exalted themselves above the knowledge of You.[2] I have become vain in my imagination.[3] I've not been diligent to renew my mind and seek to establish a new pattern of thinking according to Your truth.[4]

When I have prayed, often even when I knew I was praying within Your will, I have doubted that You would answer. Please forgive me for blaspheming Your name in this way and for spurning Your faithfulness. Thank You that You are dealing with this sin in my life and are teaching me how to combat it. O Lord, I beg for repentance to be sure and certain and deep and permanent.

You have said, "When Jesus returns, will He find faith?"[5] Let me be among those who are pleasing to You, Father (for without faith, no one can please God). I also believe, Lord, that You *are* and that You are a rewarder of those who diligently seek You.[6] It's true that if we *really* believed You are good and that Your will for our lives is always best, and that You have the power to perform it, we would never disobey. We would never have any reason to disobey.

My very actions show that I haven't really believed or trusted You. Lord, Your Word says that faith comes by hearing, and hearing by the Word of God.[7] So, as I hide Your Word in my heart and meditate upon it, You will not let Your Word return unto You void, but will perform that which You intended.[8] Thus, I can expect faith to come and vanquish unbelief.

Thank You, Father, for forgiving me, and thank You for the work You are going to do in my heart to make me a woman of faith. I believe, Lord; deal a death blow to my unbelief.[9] Cause me to be singleminded and not tossed to and fro.[10] Help me not to live by my emotions or circumstances but by the truth of Your Word.

You told the Israelites that the good news they heard did not profit them because it was not united by faith.[11] But the righteous one shall live by faith.[12] But we are not of those who shrink back to destruction but who have faith to the preserving of the soul.[13]

Lord, I feel that my greatest area of doubt or unbelief has been not letting Your power work in me to deliver me from sin. Your Word says in the last days men will hold to a form of godliness but deny the power thereof—*Your* power to work true godliness in them.[14]

Sometimes I act as if my flesh is stronger than Your Spirit or my sin is too great for You to handle. O Lord God, forgive me for doubting Your power. You have already dealt with sin through Your Son. I just need to believe it and exercise faith for victory over sin in my own life. I do believe. *You* are the source of my faith.[15]

Scripture Guide

Without becoming weak in faith [Abraham] contemplated his own body, now as good as dead since he was about a hundred years old, and the deadness of Sarah's womb; yet, with respect to the promise of God, he did not waver in unbelief, but grew strong in faith, giving glory to God, and being fully assured that what He had promised, He was able also to perform.

Romans 4:19–21

To whom did [God] swear that they should not enter His rest, but to those who were disobedient? And so we see that they were not able to enter because of unbelief.

Hebrews 3:18–19

Since therefore, brethren, we have confidence to enter the holy place by the blood of Jesus, by a new and living way which He inaugurated for us through the veil, that is, His flesh, and since we have a great priest over the house of God, let us draw near with a sincere heart *in full assurance of faith*, having our hearts sprinkled clean from an evil conscience and our bodies washed with pure water. Let us hold fast the confession of our hope without wavering, for He who promised is faithful.

Hebrews 10:19–23

Meditation Response

Is unbelief a problem for me? Have I let the traditions of men make God's Word of no effect? If so, in what ways? When and where do my doubts emerge? How do I plan to cope with this?

Neglect of Prayer

*H*ow fallow my ground must be, that I am negligent of so powerful a thing as prayer! I have heard much teaching on intercession. I have even made commitments to You, Lord, to be an intercessor, and have asked You to grant me a spirit of supplication.[1] Yet my prayer life remains such a pitiful failure; I can hardly get down to prayer for an hour at a time.

Most of my prayers are here and there, on the run, and for the most part selfish. I seem to let all other activities, the chores and cares of the world, take precedence over time in my prayer closet.

Lord, what is the matter with me? Why am I so slothful and complacent? Please forgive me and wake me up! There's no excuse for my apathetic and uncaring heart, for You have given me everything I need to overcome. Purify my motives, O Lord, and align me with Your will and purposes. Let my love for You be the motivating factor in my coming apart to be with You in prayer. Let me be used by You to be a repairer of the breach,[2] a tool used in Your hands to bring healing and to release Your power to save others.

Grant me faith and a pure heart, that I might prevail in prayer and learn what it means to pray through. Even now, Lord, as I am confronted with repentance in this area, I am more interested in going to bed than in praying for two minutes. Lord God, You are my only hope!

I'm so undisciplined. Make me willing to yield to You and to become a real prayer warrior. You've invested greatly in me, Father, and I realize the power is available to tear down the strongholds of the enemy.[3] Do all that is needed in me to help me overcome in prayer.

Lord, I will to repent of the sin of prayerlessness.[4] I rest in You and look to Your Spirit for the power to perform it. Again, my God, I ask You for the gift of genuine repentance in this area. I expect results and I put my trust in You. You are able to make all grace abound toward me so that I, having all sufficiency in all things, may abound to every good work.[5] I will devote myself to prayer and build myself up on my most holy faith, praying in the Holy Spirit.[6]

Scripture Guide

"Keep watching and praying, that you may not come into temptation; the spirit is willing, but the flesh is weak."

Mark 14:38

With all prayer and petition pray at all times in the Spirit, and with this in view, be on the alert with all perseverance and petition for all the saints.

Ephesians 6:18

Be anxious for nothing, but in everything by prayer and supplication with thanksgiving let your requests be made known to God. And the peace of God, which surpasses all comprehension, shall guard your hearts and your minds in Christ Jesus.

Philippians 4:6–7

Devote yourselves to prayer, keeping alert in it with an attitude of thanksgiving.

Colossians 4:2

Meditation Response

What priority do I give to my prayer life? How much time do I give each day to prayer? Is it enough? Am I willing to get up an hour earlier each day to pray? What else can I do to strengthen this part of my life?

Neglect of Grace

*S*o many forms of grace have You provided, Lord. There are Your Word, Your Spirit, Your blood, baptism, prayer, the Communion table, fellowship with other believers, praise, singing, and many more. Abundant grace has truly been made available to me, yet if I had given myself wholeheartedly to Your "freely given unmerited favor and love," surely I would not have continued in this wretched state.

I confess the sin of having neglected sorely all the forms of grace You have given me so freely. Let Your grace in my life, O Lord, be no longer in vain.

Thank You, O God, for Your grace, so undeserved, by which I am saved. You are able to make all grace abound toward me so that I, having all sufficiency in all things, may abound to every good work.[1]

Thank You that by Your grace I am able to be what You created me to be, to walk in all the good works which You prepared beforehand that I should walk in.[2] Help me each day, Lord, to seek You for this, to stay within the bounds of Your grace and love. I see, too, that Your grace is the availability of Your power to deliver me. I have no excuse to remain in bondage of any sort.

All my life I have been told that grace is unmerited favor, meaning that when You said to the apostle Paul, "My grace is sufficient for you," You were saying You would give Paul the grace to endure his mysterious thorn, period.[3] Yet grace is much more than that; it is powerful stuff! Grace is Your ability to do in us what we can never do alone. Grace is the desire and the power to do Your will. Grace is what makes us overcomers!

How many times I, like Paul, come to You begging for deliverance from some seemingly unbearable trial! Yet because Your work on the cross was so finally, thoroughly, and irrevocably complete, nothing needs to be added or can be added to it. You still say to us, "My grace is sufficient for you—you have everything you need in Me to overcome this thing. Go for it and see My mighty power demonstrated in your weakest areas!"

I have been waiting for You to come and do something, while You have been waiting for me to act on what You have already done! Amazing grace, saving grace, delivering grace, healing grace. Yes, Your abundant grace, simply received (along with Your gift of righteousness) causes me to reign in life through the One, Jesus Christ![4]

How kind and good You are, holy Father. Your mercies are new every morning. Great is Thy faithfulness.[5]

Scripture Guide

The free gift is not like the transgression. For if by the transgression of the one [Adam] the many died, much more did the grace of God and the gift by the grace of the one Man, Jesus Christ, abound to the many.

Romans 5:15

And the Law came in that the transgression might increase; but where sin increased, grace abounded all the more.

Romans 5:20

"My grace is sufficient for you, for power is perfected in weakness."

2 Corinthians 12:9

Let us therefore come boldly unto the throne of grace, that we may obtain mercy, and find grace to help in time of need.

Hebrews 4:16 (KJV)

Meditation Response

How has God blessed me when I have been undeserving? Do I truly believe He loves me? Is it hard for me to accept a gift from God, or anyone, that I haven't earned?

Indifference to Christian Duties

Lord, forgive me for all those times I have spurned the privilege of assembling together with my fellow believers.[1] In each case I was the loser. Forgive me for those lost opportunities to commend my pastor for a helpful sermon, to lift the spirit of a discouraged disciple, to thank the soloist, to praise the Bible teacher, to show gratitude for those Christian friends who care about me and my family. I have been so negligent in interceding for them, too.

Already I have confessed to You a lack of fervor in reading Your Word and in prayer, and I have asked Your forgiveness for this, too. Apart from You, Lord, I can keep no vow, nor can I do one good thing.[2]

Please help me understand that it is You, God, who works in me both to will and to do of Your good pleasure.[3] Work in me, O Lord, and cause me to be quick to hear and to obey—to do that which Your Spirit says.[4] Grant me repentance that I might receive Your will with a good and honest heart.[5]

Scripture Guide

"I will give you a new heart and put a new spirit within you; and I will remove the heart of stone from your flesh and give you a heart of flesh."

Ezekiel 36:26

Let us consider how to stimulate one another to love and
good deeds, not forsaking our own assembling together,
as is the habit of some, but encouraging one another; and
all the more, as you see the day drawing near.

                                                      Hebrews 10:24–25

Meditation Response

What comprises my list of lost opportunities to be an
encourager of others? Is it lassitude, or self-centeredness,
that prevents me from seeking a closer relationship with
God and fellow believers? Am I afraid that if people really
know me as I am, they will dislike or reject me?

Unconcern for the Souls of Family and Friends

O God, I hide my face in shame at the lack of concern I have shown toward my own relatives who do not seem to know You. Many days pass when I do not even think of them or utter a prayer on their behalf. I know there is a possibility that they are lost, that they do not know the purpose for their lives and may face the awful prospect of eternal hell.

What grieves me so is the fact that by my apparent lack of love for my relatives and close friends, I come across as not even caring. O Lord, please forgive my hardness of heart and lack of compassion. Plant in me a concern and even a zeal to stand in the gap for them as an intercessor, to give myself, my time, my energy to apprehend in prayer for them all that is Your will (salvation, wholeness, healing, deliverance from bondage).

Lord, some of these friends and relatives are in pain, in the midst of divorce, alienated from loved ones. Please increase Your compassion and love for them in my heart that I might love them more, through both prayer and actual contact. Do a work in my heart, Lord, that will bear fruit—fruit that will remain.[1] Thank You, O my God. Your love is shed abroad in my heart by Your Spirit for these souls.[2]

Scripture Guide

"This is My commandment, that you love one another, just as I have loved you."

John 15:12

Above all, keep fervent in your love for one another, because love covers a multitude of sins.

1 Peter 4:8

Meditation Response

What is my Christian responsibility to those close to me whom I know are unsaved? How do I pray for them? What else can I do to show my concern for them beyond prayer? What is Your strategy, Lord, for situations like this?

Unconcern for Lost Souls in the World

Lord, how could I be so apathetic to millions in the world who are bound for hell unless they believe? How could I live such a selfish life as to spend so little time praying or even thinking of those who are lost? How could I spend so much of our money on temporal, material things that will just gather dust or rust?[1]

Father, I confess that I have been guilty of all of these things and have not sacrificed or denied myself in one area on behalf of the lost. God, forgive me. Please soften my heart toward them, and put a true concern in my heart. Show me ways, Lord, that I might repent in this area. Forgive me for my selfishness and strengthen me to say no to the flesh when it tries to hinder repentance regarding care for the lost.

Lord, I ask that the truth and power of the Gospel convict me for my lack of concern for these souls, for I know that it was Your Spirit working in Paul that enabled him to say: "I have great sorrow and unceasing grief in my heart. For I could wish that I myself were accursed, separated from Christ for the sake of my brethren, my kinsmen according to the flesh."[2] Paul's concern must also have been directed to the heathen outside Israel, for his life was poured out to Jew and Gentile alike.

Father, please give me Your eternal perspective and keep me from deception and apathy. Thank You for delivering me from this sin and for showing me that when I am devoted to prayer for the lost, I am less inclined to love the things of the world.[3]

Scripture Guide

. . . He who is wise wins souls.

Proverbs 11:30b

"For God so loved the world, that He gave His only begotten Son, that whoever believes in Him should not perish, but have eternal life."

John 3:16

Meditation Response

Does praying for the salvation of millions seem a daunting, almost impossible task? How can I focus my prayers on a smaller target? Can I come up with a plan to pray for a different group of lost individuals each day?

Failure to Guard Against Discouragement

*F*ather, I confess to discouragement. In looking back, I see how little progress I have made and how little fruit has been produced in my life. I still feel such a lack of repentance and so much hardness in my heart. I still have difficulty forgiving others and I struggle so with resentment. At times I feel like giving up on my quest toward holiness, toward the goal of having a pure, undefiled heart. Oh, that I would hate sin in my life and receive Your Word with a good and honest heart![1]

I don't want simply to confess and then go on committing the same sins. I know Your Word says it is better not to vow a vow than to vow it and not keep it.[2] And yet, Lord, how often I have made promises or had good intentions only to fall back into my old ways. I should be hating all that sin You have delivered me from instead of being pulled back to it.

O God, have mercy on me. Don't take Your Holy Spirit from me.[3] Don't give up on me, though I have to admit if I were You, I would have written me off years ago. Lord, I thank You for Your longsuffering and for Your faithfulness. I thank You for Your promise that You will never leave me or forsake me.[4] Work the reality of that truth into my heart, and, Lord, please show me how to keep from forsaking You.

I resist discouragement and continue this confession only out of obedience to Your Word, trusting You to honor Your Word, that if I confess my sins, You are faithful and just to forgive my sins and to cleanse me from all unrighteousness.[5] Lord, only You can cleanse me and do a work in my heart to cause me to hate sin and see it as You do. Help me to choose to turn away from evil, to say no quickly to my flesh. You, Father, through the death and resurrection of Your Son, have set me free from the dominion of sin.[6] I *can* say no, and Your Spirit in me *is* stronger than my flesh and sin.[7]

I am only too aware of Your warning to me to watch and pray that I may not enter into temptation, for the spirit is willing but the flesh is weak.[8] Help me to do this—to watch and pray, to be sober, vigilant, on the alert for Satan and his schemes.[9] Cause me to hate him and all he stands for. Father, I see that he wants to kill, steal, and destroy all You have purchased for me, while Your Son came to give me abundant life.[10]

Help me, too, O Lord, to pursue righteousness, like the widow before the judge, with importunity—meaning pressing or urging with troublesome persistence.[11] I picture myself like Jacob, holding onto Your feet, Lord, saying, "I will not let You go unless You bless me"[12]— with deliverance from sin, sickness, fear, discouragement, demonic power.

Please help me to see and love the value of my inheritance in You, Lord, for I need You so.

Scripture Guide

"If you do well, will not your countenance be lifted up? And if you do not do well, sin is crouching at the door; and its desire is for you, but you must master it."

Genesis 4:7

"I am the vine, you are the branches; he who abides in Me, and I in him, he bears much fruit; for apart from Me you can do nothing."

John 15:5

Be steadfast, immovable, always abounding in the work of the Lord, knowing that your toil is not in vain in the Lord.

1 Corinthians 15:58

Meditation Response

How do I cope with discouragement? How do I handle setbacks in my Christian walk? When I backslide, do I have a set procedure to begin moving ahead again?

Failure to Trust God with My Children

So often I don't live out the very things I try to teach the children. I teach patience and at times am impatient. I teach honesty and come short of it myself. I teach discipline and then am undisciplined. I tell them how important prayer is, while my prayers for them are so sporadic and inadequate. Forgive me, Lord, for my hypocrisy; please make me a *doer* and not just a teacher of Your Word.[1]

Father, right now I repent of not trusting Your ability to protect our children from the spirit of this age. I seek Your will for our children. I rejoice in Your faithfulness and the knowledge that You love each of them more than we do. Therefore, with confidence, Lord, I petition You to put a hunger and thirst for Yourself in their hearts.[2] Give them understanding, that they may observe Your law and keep it with all their hearts.[3] Put the desire in them to seek You diligently,[4] while You may be found.[5] Let Your Kingdom come and Your will be done in their lives.[6] Keep them from the evil one[7] and from hidden or presumptuous sins.[8]

Because Your Word says that whatever we, Your people, bind on earth will be bound in heaven, and whatever we loose on earth will be loosed in heaven,[9] I bind in the name of Jesus any powers of darkness sent to thwart or hinder Your purposes for my children's lives. I bind any spirits of pride, rebellion, deception, or perversion. I loose

Your Spirit of humility, submission, and revelation knowledge of You, which will bring them to maturity. Satan, in Jesus' name I break your power over my children.[10] I have committed them to the Lord Jesus Christ and am persuaded that He is able to keep that which I have committed to Him until that day.[11]

Lord, You promise Your servants that our children will be taught of the Lord, and great will be their peace and undisturbed composure.[12] I put the blood of Christ, our Passover Lamb, on the doorposts and lintels of our house.[13]

Thank You, Father, that it is not Your will that any should perish, but that all should come to repentance.[14] Cause my children to be mighty men and women of God, vessels of honor for Your glory.[15] May they put Your Word first in their lives.[16] Deliver them from any lust, greed, and worldly-mindedness.[17] Teach them to fear Your awesome and holy name, for truly the fear of the Lord is the beginning of wisdom.[18]

Father, because these requests are according to Your will, I know that You have heard me and that I have the petition for which I am asking.[19] I come boldly to Your throne of grace,[20] putting You in remembrance of Your Word.[21] I say to You, Lord, "Do as You have promised." Thank You, thank You, thank You that I know I *can* trust You with my children.

Scripture Guide

Fathers [and mothers], do not provoke your children to anger; but bring them up in the discipline and instruction of the Lord.

Ephesians 6:4

Meditation Response

What kind of parental example do I set for my children? Do I trust God to cover my inadequacies and keep them from evil? Do I pray for them in faith? How do I pray for them? Where do I fail them? How can I do better?

Neglect
of Family
Duties

*L*ord, I confess that I have not made it a top priority to serve my family with joy, but often find myself seeking to be served by them. Your Word says that my husband has authority over my body[1] and I have not always honored his right here. Please change my way of thinking, Lord, so that I will joyfully prefer to meet my family's needs over my own.

What an awesome challenge to be parents in this day and age! How different a world than even twenty or thirty years ago when I was growing up. And yet, Father, Your grace is adequate for even the monumental task of maintaining a godly family today.[2]

Grant my heart's cry to have a home free from all strife[3] and ruled by Your love. I see that we must avoid strife as a poisonous snake because it stops Your power.[4] Teach me to love my family unconditionally.

Father, You are convicting me also regarding financial accountability before You. Your Word says that it is required of stewards that they be found faithful.[5] I confess to You those areas in which I have not been faithful, when I have mismanaged money, spent frivolously, eaten out too frequently, and not really known where a lot of our money was even going. How can I give an account to You under those circumstances?[6] Forgive me for this, Lord.

Thank You for giving me the most wonderful family in

all the earth, Father. May I treasure and honor and cherish them and treat them with reverence, love, and patience.

Scripture Guide

Wives, be subject to your husbands, as is fitting in the Lord. Husbands, love your wives, and do not be embittered against them. Children, be obedient to your parents in all things, for this is well-pleasing to the Lord.

Colossians 3:18–20

Review Ephesians 5:15–33.

Meditation Response

What kind of a family woman [man] am I, really? What am I neglecting in this area? What can I do about it?

Neglect
of Social
Responsibilities

*F*ather, I'm amazed at how I could be so nonchalant about what is going on in the world about me! The famine in Africa, fighting in the Middle East and Central America, earthquakes, floods. I pay so little attention to them. Even worse, I am too little concerned for the injustices done to minority groups, the homeless in or near my own community.

Am I ready to be a good Samaritan to my neighbor down the street?

I must see and accept these and other social responsibilities reflected by our founding fathers' willingness to pledge their lives, their wealth, and their sacred honor to purchase the freedoms we have come to take so for granted; and in view of Your Word, which says, "Let justice roll down like waters and righteousness like an ever-flowing stream."[1]

I shudder to think of the consequences we are now facing because we, Your people, have failed to be salt and light in our society.[2] Because we have failed to occupy till Jesus comes,[3] we now have the blood of over twenty million unborn babies on our hands, an AIDS plague, and an eight billion dollar pornography industry.

Turn our eyes, O Lord, from looking at vanity and revive us in Your ways.[4] Revive Your work in the midst of the years, in the midst of the years make it known. In Your wrath, remember mercy.[5]

Scripture Guide

"You are the salt of the earth; but if the salt has become tasteless, how will it be made salty again? It is good for nothing anymore, except to be thrown out and trampled under foot by men. You are the light of the world. A city set on a hill cannot be hidden."

Matthew 5:13–14

"Then they themselves also will answer, saying, 'Lord, when did we see You hungry, or thirsty, or a stranger, or naked, or sick, or in prison, and did not take care of You?'

"Then He will answer them, saying, 'Truly I say to you, to the extent that you did not do it to one of the least of these, you did not do it to Me.' "

Matthew 25:44–45

Meditation Response

What is the extent of my indifference regarding the injustices and hurts dealt out to minority groups? Do I want to change? How do I go about this?

Failure to Guard Against Sinful Behavior

*B*itterness, self-pity, resentment, slander, abusive speech, malice, and clamor. Lord, I am guilty of all these sins that You warn against. And Father, worst of all, I have grieved and quenched Your precious Spirit. At times a spirit of independence and rebellion in me leads me to refuse to listen to and obey Your voice. And, O Lord, what corruption all of this reaps![1]

Forgive me, Father. Help me to keep my tongue from evil and my lips from speaking guile.[2] Do a work in my heart so that I will love You so much, I'll be willing to say no to the flesh that wants to be satisfied. I will buy from You gold refined by fire[3]—the pain of letting the flesh die. Make me willing to endure this pain and draw nigh to You.

How I praise You, Lord, for granting me forgiveness, for washing me clean with Your blood and Your Word,[4] and for working in my heart to cause me to hate that kind of behavior and to love Your righteousness.[5] Lord, I know You are putting a love in my heart for You that I've never known before, and You are working willingness into my heart to deny myself so that I can better obey and serve You. You are showing me Your power to overcome and You are uniting my heart to fear Your name.[6] The fear of the Lord is to hate evil.[7] O Lord, how I praise You for doing this.

I see how Satan would take my sin and use it for evil; You are taking it and turning it to good, causing me to hate sin and all its destructive results.[8] I see what a cruel and hard taskmaster Satan is, and how he is the father of lies.[9] Lord, I pray that my spirit, where You dwell, may become strong and have dominion over all my flesh.

Lord, I confess faith in Your ability to work in me a gentle, quiet spirit,[10] slow to speak and quick to listen.[11] Give me a heart out of which will flow rivers of living water,[12] that no unwholesome word will proceed from my mouth, but only such a word as is good for edification according to the need of the moment, that it may impart grace to those who hear.[13]

Be Lord of every area of my life. Thank You, Jesus, that when You died, You nailed to the cross my rebellion, my uncircumcised heart, my haughtiness and pride, and my self-love, along with all that keeps me from Your will, all that keeps me from Your righteousness, all that keeps me from faith, all that keeps me from being made holy by You. Thank You for Your finished work and for Your power to make it a reality in my life.

Father, I exchange my heart of stone for the new heart that You put in me. You have written Your law upon it[14] that I might obey You from the heart—not by the letter, but by the Spirit. Please take my will and make it Thine.

By Your resurrected life in me, Lord, I seek to deny myself. I reckon my flesh dead to sin and alive unto God.[15] Therefore, I ask You to help me, Father, not to go on yielding the members of my body as slaves to sin, but to yield my members as slaves to righteousness through You.[16]

Cause me, O God, to hate sin in my life and to love righteousness.[17] You alone can do this, but it is Your will; therefore, I believe You hear me and that this day I have that for which I am asking You.[18] I am calling into being, by faith, that which has not existed in deed in my life,[19] but which does exist in reality because of what You did on the cross and because You were raised from the dead through the glory of the Father.[20] This reality *shall* be made manifest in my life. Hallelujah! I reckon my flesh dead to sin.[21]

Scripture Guide

Watch over your heart with all diligence, for from it flow the springs of life. Put away from you a deceitful mouth, and put devious lips far from you.

Proverbs 4:23–24

Take pains with these things; be absorbed in them, so that your progress may be evident to all. Pay close attention to yourself and to your teaching; persevere in these things; for as you do this you will insure salvation both for yourself and for those who hear you.

1 Timothy 4:15–16

Meditation Response

Am I able to resist the temptation to utter hurting words with my tongue? Is my prayer life building up inside me a strong defense against becoming angry, resentful, arrogant, filled with self-pity?

Reluctance
to Give
Correction

*L*ord, this is an area in which I greatly need Your help and discernment. There have been so many times when I have seen disobedience in the lives of my Christian friends and have not been able or willing to speak to them in love about it. Because You've shown me so much sin in my own life, I feel I have no right to judge.

At other times I have been guilty of speaking my mind too bluntly and without sensitivity. Lord, I know You've told us to remove the log from our own eye before taking the speck out of our brother's.[1] You've also told us that within the Church we are to judge with righteous judgment,[2] speaking the truth in love,[3] and watch over one another's lives, to admonish and reprove each other when needed.[4]

Please help me, Father, to grow in wisdom as to how and when to do this, and when not to. Help me to learn when correcting someone is my responsibility—and when it is not.

Scripture Guide

Faithful are the wounds of a friend, but deceitful are the kisses of an enemy.

Proverbs 27:6

71

Iron sharpens iron, so one man sharpens another.

Proverbs 27:17

Meditation Response

It is easy or hard for me to correct others? Have I lost friends by doing this? Do I have love in my heart when I correct someone else?

Neglect
of
Self-Denial

*F*ather, I come to You confessing my self-indulgent ways and self-centeredness. So often I do what I want, go where I want, eat what I want, sleep when I want. Sleep, food, pleasure are all still clamoring for first place in my life and I often allow them to take control.

I know that apart from You, Lord, there is no hope for me; but I believe that You are quite able to overcome this sin in my life. Part of the fruit of Your Spirit is self-control, and Your resurrected life in me is able to overcome self and sin. Indeed, because I belong to You, I have crucified the flesh with its evil passions and desires.[1] Thank You, Lord, that You are causing me to love You more than self, that You are making me sharply aware that in You, I am more than a conqueror.[2]

I ask, Father, that You would establish my footsteps in Your Word and not allow any sin to have dominion over me.[3] How dare I continue to act independent of You or act as if I may do as I please!

O Lord, please forgive me for spurning Your Lordship in my life. Come, Holy Spirit, and rule and reign in all these areas. Father, make me so sensitive to Your Spirit and so aware of Your ownership of me that I am careful to hear Your voice and obey, no matter what the pain to my flesh.

Father, how is it that I could so blithely ignore Your nonnegotiable terms for true discipleship? At times today it seems Your Gospel has been reduced to nothing more than a vast system of indulgences (covered by Your grace, of course) rather than what it truly is—a narrow road to the cross. I must reckon with Your words that I cannot be Your disciple unless I deny myself, take up my cross daily, and follow You![4]

Lord, please give me the gumption and determination to say no to what I want (my will), no to what I feel (my emotions), and no to what I think (my mind), so that the only thing that matters is that You have Your way. May what You want, what You feel, and what You think be accomplished and carried out in my life. Lord, to walk in this way is more than I can ask or think, but You are able to do exceedingly abundantly above all that I can ask or think.[5]

Please deliver me from my worst enemy—self-indulgence. I beg for repentance in this area. I will to repent. After hearing You for years prompting us to get out of debt, I now sense an urgency to obey You in this, and to do anything necessary to get totally free from financial bondage. The astronomical national debt is only a reflection of the greed and lust we as individual Americans have indulged in. We live in such a Disneyland compared to the rest of the world. We've failed to realize just how pervasive the idol of materialism has become.

Forgive us, Lord. We have become a nation of spiritual adulterers.[6] May we heed Your Word and consider ourselves as dead to immorality, impurity, passion, evil desire, and greed which amounts to idolatry.[7]

I see the road ahead. I am to bear the cross of the irritations and inconveniences that come every day and praise You in their midst.[8] If I suffer for doing what is right, I am to bear it patiently, trusting myself to You, my faithful Creator.[9] I am to be ready and willing to be ignored or criticized or even rejected in serving You.[10]

Father, forgive me for wanting to avoid the way of suffering and death to self. Grant me a revelation of the power of the cross.[11] Show me how to walk in holiness by faith. Give me a deeper revelation of what true faith is—that it comes from knowing and falling in love with Jesus,[12] the Living Word.[13]

Oh, that I might know You, and the power of Your resurrection, and the fellowship of Your sufferings, being conformed to Your death.[14]

Father, may I count all things as loss, even rubbish, compared to the possession of the priceless privilege—the overwhelming preciousness, the surpassing worth and supreme advantage—of knowing Christ Jesus my Lord.[15]

Scripture Guide

But I buffet my body and make it my slave, lest possibly, after I have preached to others, I myself should be disqualified.

1 Corinthians 9:27

For the love of Christ controls us, having concluded this, that one [Jesus] died for all, therefore all died; and He died for all, that they who live should no longer live for themselves, but for Him who died and rose again on their behalf.

2 Corinthians 5:14–15

For you have been called for this purpose, since Christ also suffered for you, leaving you an example for you to follow in His steps, who committed no sin, nor was any deceit

found in His mouth; and while being reviled, He did not
revile in return; while suffering, He uttered no threats, but
kept entrusting Himself to Him who judges righteously.

1 Peter 2:21–23

Meditation Response

In what areas of my life do I show self-control? What
areas are out of control? Do I shrink from denying myself?
If so, in what ways? Can I believe God for the power to
change? What is my plan?

Lack
of
the Fear
of God

O God, I tremble at how lightly I regard Your law and Your ownership of me. I tremble at the good intentions and promises I have made to You and how shallow is my real commitment. So many of my responses to You are purely emotional and not followed through on. If I truly feared You and truly believed the awesomeness of Your holiness, I would never trifle with Your Word as I do.

It is so clear in Scripture that we are to have a healthy fear of You, Lord. Some people would substitute the word *awe* for fear. That's fine, too, but I will stick with Your Word. True reverence for You necessitates obedience. It is Your kindness that leads me to repentance.[1]

So I repent now of my casual attitude toward holiness and righteousness. I repent of my shallow commitment to You. I repent of my unwillingness to take Your Word more seriously, to absorb it into my being.

Teach me to fear You, Lord.

Scripture Guide

The fear of the Lord is clean, enduring forever. . . .

Psalm 19:9a

77

"Cease striving and know that I am God."

Psalm 46:10a

"The fear of the Lord is to hate evil; pride and arrogance and the evil way, and the perverted mouth, I hate."

Proverbs 8:13

The fear of the Lord is the beginning of wisdom, and the knowledge of the Holy One is understanding.

Proverbs 9:10

The fear of the Lord prolongs life.

Proverbs 10:27a

The fear of the Lord leads to life, so that one may sleep satisfied, untouched by evil.

Proverbs 19:23

Meditation Response

How do I respond to the scriptural command to fear God? The key points of my relationship to God are as follows:

PART III

SINS
OF
COMMISSION

Ingratitude

Lord, I could write a book confessing just this one sin! Ingratitude can lead so quickly to murmuring, complaining, and discontent. Repentance of this sin is critical. I believe gratefulness truly *is* the master key that unlocks the heart of God.

Though I am especially thankful for my family, Lord, I often act ungrateful. I go days without feeling sheer joy for the gift they are to me. Though I enjoy the children so, I sometimes grumble at the chores or the mounds of work required to care for them. What would I do without all the modern conveniences?

I want to heed Your stern warning, Father, speaking about the Israelites in the wilderness who were destroyed by the destroyer because they murmured against Your dealings with them. In fact, You say explicitly that all those things happened to them as examples to us upon whom the ends of the ages have come![1]

Surely no people on earth have ever had more to be thankful for than we who live in America. But unless we know Your ways, we also will perish in our wilderness experiences—times of trial and testing. You told Moses that after You led Your people into the Sinai wilderness, You let them go hungry to humble them and test them to find out what was really in their hearts. You wanted them to learn that man does not live by bread alone, but by every word that proceeds from the mouth of God.[2]

Yet they were never satisfied with Your provision. They always lusted after their own carnal desires, including leeks, onions, garlic, and cucumbers! They murmured against Your anointed leadership and actually preferred returning to bondage under their oppressors to trusting You to bring them into the good land that You had promised. How sad that the very generation You led out of Egypt by Your mighty power, with signs and wonders, died in the wilderness never receiving its inheritance because of unbelief.[3] Their grumblings revealed the root of unbelief. Murmuring and complaining are merely the praise words of the worship of self.

Father, I repent of ingratitude, murmuring, and complaining. I seek instead to cultivate a grateful heart. Thank You for the hundreds of blessings throughout my life, many of which I have taken for granted. How many times You have protected me from disaster just by Your mercy!

Thank You for any honors I have received. Thank You for my heritage, for family and friends and relatives and teachers who have influenced my life for good.

Thank You for my health and the health of my family. Thank You for Your healing power.

Thank You for Your intimate and constant expressions of steadfast love and faithfulness.

Thank You for Your Holy Spirit and for convicting me of sin.[4] Thank You for hearing my repentant heart cry out to You.

So I ask You please to forgive my ingratitude and help me to repent of this sin. With my will, I do repent. Lord, grant me fruit in keeping with repentance.[5] And help me especially to love You for who You are and not just for all You've done for me. Thank You for Your character—Your gracious, loving nature as well as Your holiness, justice, and righteousness.

Finally, thank You, Jesus, for Your death on the cross that made it possible for mercy to triumph over judgment.[6] Thank You that You died for me while I was yet a sinner and that You do not deal with me according to my sins.[7]

Blessed am I whose sins You have blotted out,[8] never to be remembered again![9]

I'm learning that thanking You for meeting my need *before* I actually see the provision manifested is one of the strongest expressions of faith. And without faith it is impossible to please You.[10]

Scripture Guide

Thou . . . art enthroned upon the praises of Israel.

Psalm 22:3

I will bless the Lord at all times; His praise shall continually be in my mouth.

Psalm 34:1

Let those who love Thy salvation say continually, "Let God be magnified."

Psalm 70:4b

Enter His gates with thanksgiving, and His courts with praise. Give thanks to Him; bless His name.

Psalm 100:4

Meditation Response

When I think of people to whom I need to show more gratitude, the following names come to my mind:

How can I show gratitude to each person listed?

The "God" of Sleep

*F*ather, there is a sin in my life that has been a stumblingblock for years. It is an idolatrous love of sleep. I know You have ordained a certain amount of sleep to keep my body healthy and restored, but sometimes I go beyond that and make sleep (daytime or otherwise) a form of self-indulgence. It can also be my way of escaping reality and responsibility. Sometimes I feel so much a slave to sleep that it becomes my master.

Lord, I want to be honest with You. In my flesh I really don't want to give it up, so I begin by asking You to make me willing to persevere in whatever it takes to overcome this sin. My sorrow over it has been worldly sorrow and has not led to true repentance.[1]

I come to You now confessing this besetting sin and asking You to deliver me from it and grant me true repentance. In my own strength I cannot do it, but I know You can and I believe You will. Father, this day I approach Your throne by the blood of Jesus and nail this sin to Your cross where *it will die*. I will to love You more than sleep.

For the hours I've wasted because of this indulgence, I ask Your forgiveness. Father, please increase my faith that in You I am more than a conqueror[2] and that I am an overcomer.

Scripture Guide

Unto thee, O Lord, do I lift up my soul. O my God, I trust in thee: let me not be ashamed, let not mine enemies triumph over me.

Psalm 25:1–2 (KJV)

How long will you lie down, O sluggard? When will you arise from your sleep? "A little sleep, a little slumber, a little folding of the hands to rest"—and your poverty will come in like a vagabond. . . .

Proverbs 6:9–11

"Are you asleep? Could you not keep watch for one hour?"

Mark 14:37

"Awake, sleeper, and arise from the dead, and Christ will shine on you."

Ephesians 5:14

Meditation Response

Have I made a god of sleep? Does my desire for sleep sometimes prevent me from fulfilling my responsibilities? Am I addicted to daytime naps? Does a desire to sleep in the morning (or anytime) keep me from prayer? How can I change?

Worldliness

*H*ow insidious, Lord, is this sin in my life. Often I have not regarded the possessions You have given me as Yours, but have acted as though they were mine. Often I've not been generous toward others with all You've given. I have let materialism—things, clothes, houses—consume hours of time I could have spent with You.

Worse than that, Lord, I have not kept my thought life pure and unstained by the world.[1] I have watched things on television that were straight from the pit of hell—immorality, impurity, sensuality, strife, drunkenness[2]—all things that defile Your holy temple when I open myself to them by reading or watching or listening. Most of today's television programming and movies teach us to tolerate evil, while David, a man after God's own heart, resolved, "I will set no wicked thing before mine eyes."[3]

At times I have read cheap gossip columns in the paper, knowing that my mind was being anything but renewed by such filth. I have loved the world and the things of the world; I have not guarded against the lust of the flesh, the lust of the eyes, and the boastful pride of life.[4] All this while I have known that Your Word says, he who loves the world is an enemy of God.[5] Father, please forgive me.

I repent, Lord, of worldliness. With Your help, I will to set my mind on the higher things where You are seated,[6] that the treasure of my heart will be You alone, Lord, and not the things of the world.[7]

I pray that my heart will be directed toward You even as Moses' was when he refused to be called the son of

Pharaoh's daughter. He chose, rather, to endure ill treatment with the people of God, than to enjoy the passing pleasures of sin, and he considered the reproach of Christ greater riches than the treasures of Egypt; for Moses was looking to the reward—Christ Himself.[8]

Scripture Guide

> One thing I have asked from the Lord, that I shall seek: That I may dwell in the house of the Lord all the days of my life, to behold the beauty of the Lord, and to meditate in His temple.
>
> Psalm 27:4

> "Do not lay up for yourselves treasures upon earth, where moth and rust destroy, and where thieves break in and steal. But lay up for yourselves treasures in heaven, where neither moth nor rust destroys, and where thieves do not break in or steal; for where your treasure is, there will your heart be also."
>
> Matthew 6:19–21

> This is pure and undefiled religion in the sight of our God and Father, to visit orphans and widows in their distress, and to keep oneself unstained by the world.
>
> James 1:27

Meditation Response

How can I live in the world without being contaminated by it? How can I witness and respond to my non-Christian friends and co-workers without coming across as self-righteous?

Pride

Lord, this is a sin of which You have convicted me often. You say in Your Word that one of the things You really hate is a haughty spirit,[1] but that a broken and a contrite heart You will not despise.[2] I see so many symptoms of pride in my life:

When I become easily angered or offended by others.

When I find it difficult to forgive.

When I indulge myself or seek to protect myself from inconvenience or suffering.

When I crave the attention or approval of others.

When I feel hurt and bask in self-pity.

When I talk too much.

When I think I know better than others.

When I mistrust others or maintain expectations of them and then get disappointed when they are not met.

Then there is the matter of vanity. I feel convicted, Lord, at how much attention I can give to hair, clothes, and makeup. (As Charles Finney said, I spend more time decorating the outside of my body than taking care to keep my inward heart and character pure and lovely for You, who look on the heart.)

Lord, You tell me in Your Word that You oppose the proud but give grace to the humble.[3] In obedience to Your Word, I desire and will to repent of a proud and arrogant heart and I choose to humble myself before You. Lord, I know that true humility of heart would respond by obedience to You in every area, for You are the potter and I am the clay.[4]

You are Lord and King, and You have not only made me

but bought me with the price of Your most precious Son, in His blood poured out for me. Should the clay say to the potter, "Why have you made me this way?"[5] I also know from Your Word that You make some vessels of gold and silver for honor and some of wood and clay for dishonor.[6] Let me cleanse myself from wickedness, Lord, that I may be a vessel for honor, sanctified, useful to the Master, prepared for every good work.[7]

Please forgive me, Father, for the sin of pride, and help me to walk before You in humility and truth. I seek *You* to produce that in me by Your Spirit.

Scripture Guide

When pride comes, then comes dishonor, but with the humble is wisdom.

Proverbs 11:2

Only by pride cometh contention.

Proverbs 13:10 (KJV)

Pride goes before destruction, and a haughty spirit before stumbling.

Proverbs 16:18

I say to every man among you not to think more highly of himself than he ought to think; but to think so as to have sound judgment, as God has allotted to each a measure of faith.

Romans 12:3

With humility of mind let each of you regard one another as more important than himself; do not merely look out for your own personal interests, but also for the interests of others.

Philippians 2:3–4

Meditation Response

When does healthy self-esteem cross the border and become unhealthy pride? How do I guard against arrogant pride? What are some practical ways I can humble myself before You, God?

Envy

Lord, I ask that You would show me my sin in this area. I'm sure it is greater than I can see on the surface. You have blessed me in so many ways through my family, my home, and my special friends that I dare not be envious of anyone. Yet I need the convicting power of Your Spirit to expose any blind spots.

I do confess an envy of those whose hearts seem to be closer to You, who seem to be disciplined and quick to obey You, no matter the personal cost. I envy those who deal seriously with sin in their lives, who are willing to sacrifice anything to follow and obey You.

Lord, I feel so shallow and undisciplined and I get so bogged down in self. I know You have called me to be *me* and not the apostle Paul or Charles Finney or Catherine Marshall. Yet I know, Lord, that Your desire for me is that I be conformed to the image of Jesus,[1] which takes personal commitment and a willingness to deny self.[2] Please help me, Lord, and have mercy on me. Forgive my laziness and my envy of those who have shown themselves willing to pay the price. Make me willing to pay the price.

Scripture Guide

A sound heart is the life of the flesh: but envy the rottenness of the bones.

Proverbs 14:30 (KJV)

If anyone advocates a different doctrine, and does not agree with sound words, those of our Lord Jesus Christ, and with the doctrine conforming to godliness, he is conceited and understands nothing; but he has a morbid interest in controversial questions and disputes about words, out of which arise envy, strife, abusive language, evil suspicions. . . . But godliness actually is a means of great gain, when accompanied by contentment. . . . And if we have food and covering, with these we shall be content.

I Timothy 6:3–4, 6–8

But if ye have bitter envying and strife in your hearts, glory not, and lie not against the truth. . . . For where envying and strife is, there is confusion and every evil work.

James 3:14–16 (KJV)

Meditation Response

Do I understand how envy can create a poison inside me that stifles creativity and damages relationships? Am I willing to list here those people I envy—and how I intend to change?

Criticalness

*H*ow I grieve, O Lord, over the way Satan is turning Christian brothers against each other through criticism. Yet it's so easy to point the finger and self-righteously accuse others, when I need Your mercy and forgiveness for my own sin in this area. How often I have shown a critical, judgmental spirit and attitude. How often I have harbored bitterness or nurtured resentment as if these negative attitudes were friends rather than arch-enemies! Yet when I cut myself off from another part of the Body of Christ, I may be cutting myself off from the very means You are choosing to make me whole.

I guess this sin goes right along with slander. I confess I have been guilty of both, Lord. Even toward my husband, the one You have given me to love, encourage, support, and honor,[1] the one about whom I pray so often that I would do him good and not evil all the days of my life, and that his heart would be able to safely trust in me[2]—even toward him, Lord, am I often critical.

Father, I will, by the power of Your Spirit within me, to repent of this sin, that I might be slow to speak, quick to listen, and slow to anger,[3] that I would accept others as You have accepted me,[4] that I would freely extend mercy and forbearance.[5] Father, I will make it a habit of my life to speak, and with Your help even to think, only those words that are edifying, positive, and that give grace to those to whom I speak.[6] Surely, Lord, You are purifying and cleansing Your temple,[7] but part of that cleansing, I know, must include our learning to forgive one another as well as a willingness to travail until Christ be formed in all His people.[8] I marvel at Your patience with the Church as You have waited all these centuries to see the fulfillment of Jesus' high priestly prayer—that we may all be one even as He and the Father are one.[9] I know that unity will never come, Lord, until we repent of criticalness,[10] and that it will not be done by might or by power, but by Your Spirit.[11]

Scripture Guide

Let all bitterness and wrath and anger and clamor and slander be put away from you, along with all malice. And be kind to one another, tender-hearted, forgiving each other, just as God in Christ also has forgiven you.

Ephesians 4:31–32

And so, as those who have been chosen of God, holy and beloved, put on a heart of compassion, kindness, humility, gentleness and patience; bearing with one another, and forgiving each other, whoever has a complaint against anyone; just as the Lord forgave you, so also should you.

Colossians 3:12–13

Therefore you are without excuse, every man of you who passes judgment, for in that you judge another, you condemn yourself; for you who judge practice the same things.

Romans 2:1

Brethren, even if a man is caught in any trespass, you who are spiritual, restore such a one in a spirit of gentleness; each one looking to yourself lest you too be tempted.

Galatians 6:1

Meditation Response

Some people often excuse their harsh tongues by calling their criticism an "evaluation." Do I deceive myself this way? Have I a method of checking my critical tongue before it is loosed?

Lying

O Lord my God, how severely You treat lying in Your Word! You list liars with adulterers, homosexuals, and the like, and say that no liar will inherit Your Kingdom.[1] How lightly I have treated a sin that You hate so much! I hardly know how to begin to confess the numerous deceptive acts and ways of my life. How quickly and thoughtlessly I exaggerate to make my point, to impress others. At times I have misrepresented the truth; at other times I have told outright, blatant lies.

Often I have colored the truth to make myself look better. I think right now of incidents from the past for which I don't think I've ever asked Your forgiveness. Thank You for prompting me to confess these to You and for convicting me of these sins.

At times, Father, I have neglected to do certain things, using lies for excuses when I was embarrassed or ashamed to admit my real reason for not doing them—pure laziness. Then there have been times when I have lied about what I paid for certain things to give the impression I was spending less money than I actually was.

Forgive me for all this, Lord. Without You, my heart is deceitful above all things and desperately wicked; who can know it, but You?[2]

Father, I plead with You to remove any false way from me and graciously guide me to choose the truthful way, so that I would cultivate faithfulness and walk uprightly before You.

Scripture Guide

How blessed is he whose transgression is forgiven, whose sin is covered! How blessed is the man to whom the Lord does not impute iniquity, and in whose spirit there is no deceit!

When I kept silent about my sin, my body wasted away through my groaning all day long. For day and night Thy hand was heavy upon me; my vitality was drained away as with the fever-heat of summer. I acknowledged my sin to Thee, and my iniquity I did not hide; I said, "I will confess my transgressions to the Lord"; and Thou didst forgive the guilt of my sin.

Psalm 32:1–5

Do not lie to one another, since you laid aside the old self with its evil practices.

Colossians 3:9

God is light, and in Him there is no darkness at all. If we say that we have fellowship with Him and yet walk in the darkness, we lie and do not practice the truth; but if we walk in the light as He Himself is in the light, we have fellowship with one another, and the blood of Jesus His Son cleanses us from all sin.

1 John 1:5–7

Meditation Response

On a scale of one to ten, with ten being purity from any deceit, how do I rate myself in regard to lying? Can I acknowledge any specific situations in which my lies were self-protective? Destructive to relationships?

Cheating

*H*ere again, Lord, the instances of my guilt are many. I know the enemy would like to have me make generalizations or be vague, so I ask You to convict me here of specifics.

I know that I cheat You each day of time that should be spent with You. All the time I have on this earth is a gift from You; I have wasted so much time that is rightly Yours. Please help me to learn to use my time wisely and with reverence.

I see something else here in regard to time: When I am late to appointments, I am cheating those people of their time who have to wait for me.

I have considered selling an item to someone else for a higher price than I paid for it (since I got it at a bargain). Then You nudged me and I lowered my price. A little thing, I know, but the principle is not small.

Each time I speak negatively about anyone else, I am somehow reducing them in stature, thus cheating them.[1]

Any time I fail to give at least a tithe of my time, talent, and possessions, I am cheating You, Lord. The truth is that all I am and have belongs to You.

Scripture Guide

So teach us to number our days, that we may present to Thee a heart of wisdom.

Psalm 90:12

Righteousness and justice are the foundation of His throne.

Psalm 97:2b

Differing weights are an abomination to the Lord, and a false scale is not good.

Proverbs 20:23

Meditation Response

Since many forms of cheating are subtle and deprive others of something, do I tend to rationalize about my own actions in this area? Am I willing to list my acts that are suspect? Will I ask the Lord now to nudge me or correct me when I slip?

Hypocrisy

Omy God, how often have I seen this in my life. I have confessed sins, asked for forgiveness and deliverance, knowing all the time that true repentance was not in my heart and that I would continue in that sin. I have purposely avoided the real determination or resolve to change, the firm decision to break with that sin.

How often I have tried to impress others that I am spiritual or knowledgeable or a deep follower of Yours, knowing only too well the shallowness, disobedience, and sloppiness of my life. How little time I really spend before You, seeking You and Your Word, interceding for others. I am especially convicted of my hypocrisy in demanding performance and behavior in my children and others that I do not come anywhere near doing myself. O Lord, how You condemn these things in Your Word. Truly in many ways I have been and am a Pharisee.

God, have mercy on me and grant me true godly sorrow that leads to repentance.[1] I have often tried to conceal my sins from others. I have made excuses that were untrue in order to avoid doing something I was too lazy or just didn't want to do. I have taught principles from Your Word or delivered strong words to others, then ignored them myself. Often I have exaggerated or misrepresented facts about my life. I have shown a lack of mercy to others when I have committed the same sins, or far worse.

Lord, I look to You alone to produce a pure heart in me, for only You can change my heart. I have not done my part in keeping my heart with all diligence, although out of it flow the issues of life.[2] I have allowed my heart to be defiled time and again by thoughts, actions, and words.

Lord, I realize there is no virtue in only recognizing my sin and confessing it; this is only the first step. I must believe and trust You to cleanse me from the sin of hypocrisy. Increase my faith. Lord, I do believe; help my unbelief.[3]

Scripture Guide

Let love be without hypocrisy. Abhor what is evil; cling to what is good.

Romans 12:9

Let us draw near with a *sincere heart* in full assurance of faith, having our hearts sprinkled clean from an evil conscience and our bodies washed with pure water.

Hebrews 10:22

Meditation Response

How do I rate myself here (with a ten being completely free of hypocrisy)? When is my behavior especially suspect? Am I working on an overall plan, or on some kind of Christian walk that will lead me to a purer and more holy life?

Robbing God

I am stricken by all the ways I steal from You, Lord. Forgive me for all the times I have not even given You a thought; for the prayer times in which I let my thoughts go to worldly matters.

Forgive me for the blindness and pride of not wanting to use money we were "giving to God" to help a relative in need. Oh, how I am pierced to read of the Pharisees who would never touch that which was *corban*—set aside for God[1]—and yet neglected the weightier matters of the law—faith and mercy and justice.[2]

Lord, there is so much religiosity in me. I am careful to tithe, and am concerned about where we give our money. Yet I spend money lavishly on the family and then act regretful not to have more for the poor and needy. Lord, please help me to discipline my spending.

I know only too well Your commandment to Your children that we love You with all our minds and hearts and strength. Yet I know I rob You of my love, rightfully Yours, and withhold it.

Forgive me, Lord, for robbing You of time, money, and love. Forgive me for my rebellious spirit. Deliver me, Lord, and do a work in me so that I would truly humble myself before You. I choose humility and ask You to deal with my pride and rebellion. I bind those spirits of pride and rebellion. I speak to them as mountains and say, "Be removed from me and be cast into the sea, in Jesus' name."[3]

Scripture Guide

"Will a man rob God? Yet you are robbing Me! But you say, 'How have we robbed Thee?' In tithes and offerings. You are cursed with a curse, for you are robbing Me, the whole nation of you! Bring the whole tithe into the storehouse, so that there may be food in My house, and test Me now in this," says the Lord of hosts, "if I will not open for you the windows of heaven, and pour out for you a blessing until it overflows."

Malachi 3:8, 10

Nevertheless, the firm foundation of God stands, having this seal, "The Lord knows those who are His, " and, "Let everyone who names the name of the Lord abstain from wickedness." Now in a large house there are not only gold and silver vessels, but also vessels of wood and of earthenware, and some to honor and some to dishonor. Therefore, if a man *cleanses himself* from these things, he will be a vessel for honor, sanctified, useful to the Master, prepared for every good work. Now flee from youthful lusts, and pursue righteousness, faith, love and peace, with those who call on the Lord from a pure heart.

2 Timothy 2:19–22

Meditation Response

If I fail to tithe, could that be the source of problems and struggles in other areas?

Have I ever considered myself as robbing God? How does this apply to me—with specifics? What am I going to do to change?

Bad Temper

Where do I begin, Lord? I am not the "victim" (occasionally or otherwise) of a bad disposition. Nor is bad temper a trait I can do little about. I know that Your Spirit is given to us in order that we may overcome or put to death these ugly, moody ways. You are quite able to transform our bad temperaments.

All my life I have reacted to situations out of proportion to their significance, just as a child learns to manipulate others by pouting, harsh words, temper tantrums. I hate the way this trait has controlled me and brought misery to those I love the most. Even now, Lord, I find when I least expect it, that same ugly thing can raise its head and cause me to act like a spoiled child.

The truth is, I *choose* to let a certain thing upset me. I feed it and nurture it. O God, forgive me and change me. Make me hate the sin that so easily besets me.[1] And, Lord, when crises and tests come and I'm not prepared, please help me to be rational and not lose my temper without weighing the consequences. Help me to fear You and choose life.[2] You tell me to watch and pray that I might not enter into temptation,[3] so Lord, I have no excuse to be caught unprepared.

If I abide in You, then I am always prepared to resist any temptation or sin. Please deliver me from this satanic, fleshly pattern of behavior, and enable me to walk in Your grace to overcome it. I determine with all my will to do this.

Lord, I am ready to lay down my life for You and for my husband and children. Keep me in Your way—sensitive to

Your Spirit and loving You so that I will not hurt You by my ill temper. Forgive me for the way I've treated my family, my friends. Have mercy on me, Lord.

Scripture Guide

Establish my footsteps in Thy word, and do not let any iniquity have dominion over me.

Psalm 119:133

Do not associate with a man given to anger; or go with a hot-tempered man, lest you learn his ways, and find a snare for yourself.

Proverbs 22:24–25

An angry man stirs up strife, and a hot-tempered man abounds in transgression.

Proverbs 29:22

Be angry, and yet do not sin; do not let the sun go down on your anger.

Ephesians 4:26

See to it that no one comes short of the grace of God; that no root of bitterness springing up causes trouble, and by it many be defiled.

Hebrews 12:15

Meditation Response

Am I labeled in any sense an angry or moody person? Do I keep my anger bottled up? How do I apply my Christian faith to the negative emotions I feel? What are some healthy ways to deal with anger?

Hindering the Good Influence of Others

The main way I have been guilty of this sin is by speaking unkind words about certain people, thereby lessening their influence in other lives. Forgive me, Lord, for judging others and for passing along negatives not only about my own relatives and friends, but even about my family.

I confess, too, that I have used up the time of others in wasteful pursuits, thereby hindering them from being more useful and productive.

At times, I have hurt loved ones by my anger or criticism or lack of patience, making them insecure and less effective. Forgive me, Lord.

Scripture Guide

"Woe to the world because of its stumbling blocks! For it is inevitable that stumbling blocks come; but woe to that man through whom the stumbling block comes!"

Matthew 18:7

Let us not judge one another anymore, but rather determine this—not to put an obstacle or a stumbling block in a brother's way.

Romans 14:13

Meditation Response

I need to ask myself, how much do I care whether I increase or decrease the good another person can do? As a sin, it is on the subtle side, because we seldom know the result of our influence, good or bad, on another person. Who are the people I most influence in a negative way? in a positive way?

PART IV

ON
TO
HIGHER
GROUND

A New Beginning

Thank You, Lord, that we can always begin anew in the Christian life. Some time ago I embarked upon a period of repentance. As honestly as I know how I have laid out all my sins before You. How I praise You for Your patience with me during these weeks! I feel a tremendous weight has been removed since I have begun tearing down idols and strongholds in my life.

Time after time I had allowed myself to be deceived by the enemy, but now I am on the way to obtaining Your victory over the sin of letting love of anything but You be god in my life. Thank You for showing me the control these things have had over me.

I have not reasoned that Your purpose for me, Lord, is true freedom and joy and wholeness, and not exhaustion or frustration or lack of fulfillment. Here it is again—the same lie as in the garden![1] I see now that if I, in obedience to You, sacrifice anything You have put Your finger on as disobedience, not only will You provide the power and ability for me to overcome that temptation, once I set my will to obey,[2] but what You give me in return is so much more satisfying than the thing I sacrifice. Oh, to learn that all that really matters is pleasing You anyway, no matter what the pain to my flesh.

Another revelation—Your grace teaches me to say no to

ungodliness and fleshly desires.[3] I must remember that only to my human nature do the commandments of God seem difficult or grievous—but immediately, as I obey, Your Spirit makes them become divinely easy, because of grace. I must be careful to let Your grace teach me and not refuse it. Accomplish that in me, O God.

The picture became clearer—not only do You want to give me victory over this one area, or that area; but Your plan deals with me as a whole person. You want me free indeed!

I continue to need Your grace in so many areas, Lord— lack of discipline in the area of eating; too much sugar and too many sweets; almost no exercise. All this adds up to sloth. Winning victory in these areas will start me on a whole new lifestyle, designed by You, not me. As I get these physical areas under Your Lordship, then I will have the time and motivation to be of use to You for whatever Your purpose or pleasure would be. You want me fit to be broken bread and poured-out wine to feed and nourish others.

Therefore, I make a decision this day to begin to use the weapons supplied me by the Holy Spirit to overcome the sins of gluttony and sloth. I commit myself to glorify You in my body. And I purpose here and now to bring every area of my life into subjection to You and under the dominion of the Holy Spirit. I purpose to love You, Lord, more than any other thing.

Father, as I set my will to obey You, until the root of the wrong habits is cut, I pray that You will make me willing at the deepest level to be teachable. Help me to say no. Keep me from the evil one. You are my only hope. You are the God of hope and a strong anchor for my soul. In You I am ready to move ahead.

Scripture Guide

The Lord is my rock and my fortress and my deliverer, my
God, my rock, in whom I take refuge; my shield and the
horn of my salvation, my stronghold.

Psalm 18:2

If Thy law had not been my delight, then I would have
perished in my affliction. I will never forget Thy precepts,
for by them Thou hast revived me.
O how I love Thy law! It is my meditation all the day.

Psalm 119:92–93, 97

Meditation Response

What would a fresh start mean in my life? In what
additional areas do I need to change? Where do I want
to go?

Prayer
of
Agreement*

To continue my new walk with You, Lord, I am making this Agreement for the purpose of putting to death those habits and sins in my life that have robbed me of my inheritance as a child of God. And I am making this Agreement to open the door for Your healing power and deliverance from these besetting sins. I claim Your grace and power to overcome, and Your wisdom for a plan of victory. I purpose in my heart to allow You to change these habits, and I claim the fruit of the Spirit of self-control because Your Spirit lives in me.[1]

I agree to apply Your Word for overcoming, and if I lose one battle, I will still claim Your strength to win the war over gluttony and idolatry. I agree to spend [specify an amount of time] each day before Your throne in prayer, for Your Word admonishes me to watch and pray that I might not enter into temptation, for the spirit is willing but the flesh is weak.[2]

I praise You for Your grace and faithfulness that have enabled me to spend time each day in Your Word. This has been one of the richest blessings of my life. By it, my knowledge of You and faith in You have brought me to this Prayer of Agreement. As I learn of You and continue to behold You, I am being transformed into Your image

* For you and your prayer partner, if you have one.

from glory to glory.[3] I further commit myself to spend [specify a new amount of time] each day in Your Word.

Satan, I notify you in Jesus' name that as of this day, according to this agreement, my prayer partner and I render you helpless in your efforts to defeat us. You will not operate in the lives of us or our children. You will not harass or in any way intimidate us, because we make this pact in the name of the Lord Jesus Christ, who came to earth in the flesh and rose from the grave victorious to put to death your deeds. We are in union with Jesus; our victory over you, therefore, is in Him and is sure!

My prayer partner has read this contract and agrees with me for that victory in my life. He/she agrees to support me in prayer and action. In keeping with Matthew 18:19—"If two of you agree on earth about anything that they may ask, it shall be done for them by my Father who is in heaven"—we claim together that victory is ours over bad habits and besetting sins, agreeing in the name of Jesus according to John 16:23.

Signed,

_____   _____

Meditation Response

What amount of time is God prompting me to spend each day in prayer? in His Word? Am I willing to commit myself to rising earlier each day for these times with Him? Am I willing to agree with another believer for victory in my life?

The Law
of
Love

Lord, You are showing me that the whole Law is fulfilled in one word, *love*, and that all other pursuits in my life will be in vain unless I apprehend Your *agape* love. What an awesome thought that I could speak in every tongue, have the gift of prophecy, understand all mysteries, have all knowledge, have faith to remove mountains, give all my possessions to feed the poor, and even give my body to be burned; yet if my motive for doing all these things is not love, it will amount to one big zero![1]

Yet this very kind of love, Lord, is not an option but Your *commandment*—one of the two great commandments.[2] I'm reminded of Your words to Your people through Moses, that "this commandment is not too difficult for you, nor is it out of reach . . . but the word is very near you, in your mouth and in your heart, that you may observe it."[3] You even go so far as to say that if we abide in You and love one another, we will be perfected in Your love.[4]

Abba Father, I cry out to You in faith that You will perfect me in Your love.

I insert my name into the following verses in place of the word *love* and confess them to You, since You are love and I am born of You.[5]

Love endures long and is patient and kind; love never is envious nor boils over with jealousy; is not boastful or vainglorious, does not display itself haughtily. It is not conceited—arrogant and inflated with pride; it is not rude (unmannerly), and does not act unbecomingly. Love . . . does not insist on its own rights or its own way, for it is not self-seeking; it is not touchy or fretful or resentful; it takes no account of the evil done to it—pays no attention to a suffered wrong. It does not rejoice at injustice and unrighteousness, but rejoices when right and truth prevail. Love bears up under anything and everything that comes, is ever ready to believe the best of every person; its hopes are fadeless under all circumstances and it endures everything [without weakening]. Love never fails. . . .

1 Corinthians 13:4–8a (TAB)

Scripture Guide

Eagerly pursue and seek to acquire [this] love—make it your aim, your great quest. . . .

1 Corinthians 14:1a, TAB

Put on love, which is the perfect bond of unity.

Colossians 3:14

The goal of our instruction is love from a pure heart and a good conscience and a sincere faith.

1 Timothy 1:5

We love, because He first loved us. . . . And this commandment we have from Him, that the one who loves God should love his brother also.

1 John 4:19, 21

Meditation Response

Do I act as though love is a commandment, not an option? How can I begin to love those I have trouble loving? What can I do in my own sphere to bring about the unity of love in the Body of Christ?

The Power of My Words

What an awesome thought, Lord, to realize the value You place on our words! Truly death and life are in the power of the tongue.[1] I also know according to Your Word that there is an inseparable connection between my tongue and my heart.[2]

I acknowledge, Lord, that only after I agree with and confess what Your Word says about my condition apart from Your grace do I open the door to Your glorious, liberating light. You will go away and return to Your place until I acknowledge my guilt and seek Your face.[3] On the other hand, my faith is made effective by the acknowledging of every good thing that is in me in Christ Jesus.[4]

As I allow the light of Your Word to shine on the hidden areas of sin in my life, I will become increasingly free and cleansed.[5]

I acknowledge that there is power, Father, in confessing or "returning" Your Word to You in any area, whether regarding sin, sickness, fear, protection of my children, or anything else. You promise that Your Word will not *return* unto You void, but it shall accomplish that which You please.[6] Help me to *return* it to You in faith through my mouth so that it will succeed in the matter for which You send it.

Jesus is the High Priest of my confession,[7] and I desire to offer up a sacrifice of praise to God—the fruit of my lips that gives thanks to His name.[8] Jesus even said that by my words I shall be justified and by my words I shall be condemned.[9]

I am learning, Lord, that when I choose to speak faith-filled words, Your words, instead of words of fear, doubt, and unbelief, all the fiery darts of the enemy are quenched as You promised.[10]

You speak in Your Word about removing mountains,[11] and You also promise that whatsoever things I ask in prayer, *believing*, I shall receive.[12]

Father, in the name of Jesus, I now speak to the mountains of physical infirmity, doublemindedness, unbelief, fear, and idolatry in my life, and I say to these mountains, "Be removed from me and be cast into the sea!" I do not doubt in my heart, but I believe that what I say will happen. Thank You for Your promise that I will have what I say.[13]

Please show me, Lord, if I am harboring any unforgiveness in my heart, since I know this will block Your promise to remove these mountains.[14]

Truly Satan is after my tongue! I know that the words I speak can actually determine my destiny.[15]

Mighty Holy Spirit, come and tame my tongue! Help me not to continue to be snared by the words of my mouth. Any time I use my tongue in a way not glorifying to You, I know I am perverting Your original purpose for giving me that member. But oh, the power of ordering my way aright and offering You the sacrifice of thanksgiving! You promise to show me Your salvation.[16]

I will fill my mouth throughout this day with Your Word and affirm what You have already said is forever settled in heaven![17]

Scripture Guide

The word is very near you, in your mouth and in your heart, that you may observe it.

Deuteronomy 30:14

"The mouth speaks out of that which fills the heart."

Matthew 12:34b

"Truly I say to you, whoever says to this mountain, 'Be taken up and cast into the sea,' and does not doubt in his heart, but believes that what he says is going to happen, it shall be granted him."

Mark 11:23

If you confess with your mouth Jesus as Lord, and believe in your heart that God raised Him from the dead, you shall be saved; for with the heart man believes, resulting in righteousness, and with the mouth he confesses, resulting in salvation.

Romans 10:9–10

Meditation Response

What "mountains" need removing in my life? Will I address them directly, as God's Word commands, rather than complain *about* them—to God or to anyone who will listen? Will I allow the Holy Spirit to tame my tongue?

The Power
of a Biblical
Fast

Lord, as I think about fasting, I find it inconceivable that in years of going to church I can scarcely remember hearing one sermon on the subject of fasting. Or did I just not have ears to hear? How can anything so powerful be virtually ignored by so many Christians? Satan must know only too well how You set people free through the power of fasting.

It shouldn't surprise me that any requirement for self-denial is so often avoided by our sophisticated twentieth-century Church. Yet fasting is no manipulative tool to wrench something from Your hand that You are reluctant to give. According to Your Word, fasting is a means of humbling myself before You, of quieting my flesh so that I can hear what You are saying.

I know my motive is all-important, Lord. Let me not be like the Pharisees who fasted twice a week but totally missed what You were after.[1] Keep me from fasting self-righteously, Lord, and to be seen by men.[2] Whether I go on a liquid fast or a total fast, for one day or forty, please help me keep my heart attitude before You pure.

Let me learn, O Father, from Your Son, who seemed to take for granted that His people would fast.[3] Let me follow His pattern for fasting: in secret, and to the Father, so that You can reward us openly.[4]

He told His disciples that some evil spirits could never

be delivered except by prayer and fasting.[5] He marveled at the unbelief of His disciples, which prevented them from casting a demon out of a certain young boy.[6] Though most Scripture expositors interpret those verses to mean that Jesus was referring to the evil spirit when He said, "This kind does not go out except by prayer and fasting," He may just as well have been referring to their unbelief—that this kind of *unbelief* does not go out except by prayer and fasting.

You provide scores of other examples in Your Word, Lord, of Your miraculous intervention in the affairs of men, when they humbled themselves by fasting. But the most powerful account of the rewards You promise if we fast the fast You choose is found in Isaiah 58.

There are conditions to meet, like dividing our bread with the hungry and bringing the homeless poor into our house. When we see the naked, we are to cover him, and not to hide ourselves from our own flesh. We must remove the yoke (of legalism) from our midst, and the pointing of the finger (criticism), and speaking wickedness (cynicism). We must give that with which we sustain our own lives to the hungry and satisfy the needs of the afflicted.

Then comes the good news: the rewards far outweigh the cost!

You promise to loose us from the bonds of wickedness, to undo the bands of the yoke, to let the oppressed go free, and to break *every* enslaving yoke. Our light will break out like the dawn and our recovery will spring forth speedily. Our righteousness will go before us and Your glory will be our rear guard.

You will answer us when we call and will continually guide us and satisfy our desires. Our light will rise in darkness and our gloom will become like midday. You will give strength to our bones and we will be like watered gardens.

Those from among us will rebuild the ancient ruins and

be called repairers of the breach, the restorers of the streets in which to dwell.

Grant me the grace, O God, to fast the fast You choose.

Scripture Guide

So he was there with the Lord forty days and forty nights; he did not eat bread or drink water. And he wrote on the tablets the words of the covenant, the Ten Commandments.

Exodus 34:28

And Jesus said to them, "The attendants of the bridegroom cannot mourn as long as the bridegroom is with them, can they? But the days will come when the bridegroom is taken away from them, and then they will fast."

Matthew 9:15

Then, when they had fasted and prayed and laid their hands on [Barnabas and Saul], they sent them away.

Acts 13:3

Meditation Response

What does fasting mean to me? How often in my life have I fasted? In what ways is it important to my Christian walk? Is God leading me to make a particular commitment in this area?

A Time for War

You have made it clear to Your children, Lord, that we can expect attacks from Satan, especially when we are active for You.[1] I praise You that You have not left us defenseless in our struggle against dark powers and principalities,[2] even while You warn that Your people are destroyed for lack of knowledge![3] So often we fail to know and use Your weapons of victory over all our enemies. I thank You today for giving us the weapons to wage spiritual warfare.

Praise You, Jesus, that You came to set the captives free.[4] When You stripped Satan of his authority at Calvary, he lost all hope of ruling over mankind—unless he could keep us in deception, sin, and fear. If we choose to believe we are still the slaves of sin so long as we are in these bodies, he will be glad to accommodate us!

I know from Your Word, Lord, that we are *not* slaves of sin,[5] nor are You the accuser of the brethren. Satan is.[6] In fact, he is busy at work devising carefully thought out schemes and plots to keep us in his grip. He steadily weaves deceptive webs of intimidation, discouragement, and confusion. Unless we learn from You how to counteract his methods, we remain prisoners of war in our very own Promised Land.

Whenever Satan tries to tempt me with fear or condemnation, I remind him in no uncertain terms that I am free! I say, "Oh no, you don't, Satan," and I pull out my double-edged sword[7] and pierce him through with Psalm 27:1 and a few dozen other verses like it.

The Lord is my light and my salvation; whom shall I fear? The Lord is the defense of my life; whom shall I dread?

Psalm 27:1

Who will bring a charge against God's elect? God is the one who justifies; who is the one who condemns? Christ Jesus is He who died, yes, rather who was raised, who is at the right hand of God, who also intercedes for us.

Romans 8:33–34

[I] have come to know and have believed the love which God has for [me]. God is love, and . . . there is no fear in love; but perfect love casts out fear.

1 John 4:16, 18

Then I go and read Ephesians 6:10–18, which tells me to clothe myself each day not only with the new person I am in Christ Jesus, but with every piece of armor He has provided. Not one piece is unnecessary!

Thus, I put on the belt of truth, for Jesus, You are the way, the truth, and the life.[8]

I guard my heart with the breastplate of righteousness, as well as of faith and love.[9] Father, You made Him who knew no sin to be sin on my behalf, that I might be made the righteousness of God in Him.[10]

Even my feet are made beautiful on the mountain by the shoes of peace, as I go forth as Your ambassador, reconciling men to God through the blood of Your Son.[11]

I hold up the shield of faith, which is able to quench all the fiery darts of the evil one. Those flaming missiles are the constant thoughts hurled at my mind, which exalt themselves above the knowledge of Your nature, Lord. I will bring these thoughts captive to the obedience of Christ by replacing them with Your truth.[12]

I put on the helmet of salvation as I let my mind dwell on those things that are true, honorable, right, pure, lovely, excellent, praiseworthy, and of good repute.[13] This helmet is the helmet of hope[14]—the forerunner of faith. I know from Your Word, Lord, that faith is the substance of things hoped for and the evidence of things not seen.[15] Father, You are the God of hope who fills me with all joy and peace in believing, that I may abound in hope through the power of Your Holy Spirit.[16]

Finally, Lord, I take the sword of Your Spirit, which is the Word of God. I can fight the devil and win every time with the words *It is written!* Jesus Himself defeated Satan with these three powerful words.[17]

Nor do I omit praying at all times with all prayer and petition in the Spirit, and being on the alert with all perseverance and petition for all saints.[18]

I know, too, Lord, that Your saints overcome Satan because of the blood of the Lamb and the word of their testimony.[19] Thank You for these powerful weapons.

Thank You, Father, for the power of praise and worship, which can open prison doors and cause chains to fall off.[20]

Lord, when I am in a tight spot and don't have time to fast or even pray, just the mention of Your name with all its authority causes all hell to tremble. Praise be to the wonderful name of Jesus which is above every name.[21] Your name, Lord Jesus, is above everything—fear, cancer, sin, demons, financial need, rebellious children, depression—anything I can name.

Knowing Your names in Scripture, Lord—and thus knowing who You are, since Your name reveals Your character—causes me to fall in love with You more and more deeply, to return to You as my first love. Your name, Jesus, is as ointment poured forth.[22]

According to Your Word, Lord, You are my Provider.[23] You are my Banner of Love and Victory.[24] You are my Peace.[25] You are my Healer.[26] You are my Sanctifier.[27] You are my Shepherd.[28] You are my Righteousness.[29] You are my Present Help; You are *there*.[30]

Glorify Your name through Your people, O Lord. Yes, glorify Your name in all the earth.

Scripture Guide

The kings of the earth did not believe, nor did any of the inhabitants of the world, that the adversary and the enemy could enter the gates of Jerusalem.

Lamentations 4:12

"Simon, Simon, behold, Satan has demanded permission to sift you like wheat; but I have prayed for you, that your faith may not fail; and you, when once you have turned again, strengthen your brothers."

Luke 22:31–32

Be of sober spirit, be on the alert. Your adversary, the devil, prowls about like a roaring lion, seeking someone to devour. But resist him, firm in your faith.

1 Peter 5:8–9

Meditation Response

Have I put on God's armor to resist the evil one? Do I use it every day? How can I combat the onslaughts of evil powers and principalities?

Rejecting Satan's Lies

*F*ather, I am seeing more and more clearly why You hate lying and deceitfulness with such a violent hatred. It is because they proceed from the very nature of Satan himself, the father of lies.[1] You hate it when I lie, and You hate it when I *believe* a lie.

It seems curious to me that I have not seen until now that almost every problem in my life can be traced to believing a lie of Satan. I realize now, Father, that accepting only one lie can lead to a downward spiral of confusion and despair. And without Your mercy I would remain in that pit.

Father, You have said that if we abide in Your Word, then we will know the truth and the truth will make us free.[2] I will to cease now from believing anything contrary to Your Word. For if Satan can get me to look at my circumstances and doubt the veracity of Your Word, then I am cutting myself off from Your mercy.

Lord, Your Word promises me abundant life in every area.[3] But if I put more confidence in what is going on around me than in Your promises, then I am believing a lie.

Father, Your Word promises financial blessing if we are faithful and obedient stewards.[4] If I let a financial deficit cause me to doubt Your faithfulness to supply my needs abundantly, then I am believing a lie.

You have commanded me to love others and desire that

I let Your Spirit love through me.[5] If I become frustrated and discouraged with my inability to love as You command, then I am believing a lie.

Your Word promises that the seed of the righteous shall be delivered[6] and that You will pour out Your Spirit on our offspring and Your blessings on our descendants.[7] If I bite my fingernails and lose sleep because my children aren't presently where they need to be in You, then I am believing a lie.

Father, You have said that we are healed by Jesus' stripes.[8] If all kinds of symptoms tempt me to believe the worst and I don't cling to the truthfulness of Your Word, then I am believing a lie.

Father, I confess that I have been snared by these and other lies. I ask Your forgiveness for not trusting Your Word to be true, fully and completely. Please help me be quick to recognize lies, and to reject them by the power of the Word. I have often acted according to the philosophy "Seeing is believing." Help me, Lord, to believe Your Word before I see it accomplished—just because You said it.[9]

Thank You, precious Jesus, for Your gracious kindness toward me. In Your name I rebuke and resist the doubts and fears with which Satan would try to assail me. I stand firmly on Your Word, knowing that it cannot fail.

Scripture Guide

Keep deception and lies far from me.

Proverbs 30:8

They that observe lying vanities forsake their own mercy.

Jonah 2:8, KJV

"And everything you ask in prayer, believing, you shall receive."

Matthew 21:22

And we desire that each one of you show the same
diligence so as to realize the full assurance of hope until the
end, that you may not be sluggish, but imitators of those
who through faith and patience inherit the promises.

Hebrews 6:11–12

Meditation Response

What kinds of lies do I believe? What things make me
worried or fearful? The next time I hear a lie, will I make
the effort to respond with a promise from Scripture—and
hold it fast?

Wholeness through God's Word

Lord, I feel for the first time in my life that I am being made whole. I sense Your healing on a deep level through Your Word and by Your Spirit.

Your Word has been like a rock to me, Lord. What would I do without Your precious Word? You have promised that no temptation or trial will overtake me but such as is common to man. And You are faithful. You do not allow me to be tempted above that which I am able, but with every test You show me the way of escape, that I may be able to bear it.[1]

I am full of praise this morning, Lord. I praise You that You are the same yesterday, today, and forever.[2] That You still go about doing good and healing all those who are oppressed by the devil.[3] You came to destroy his works[4] and You were successful when You spoiled principalities and powers, triumphing over them openly.[5]

You desire above all things that I will prosper and be in health even as my soul prospers.[6] My soul does prosper as I renew my mind in Your Word.[7] You bore my sins in Your body on the cross that I might die to sin and live to righteousness, for by Your stripes I was healed.[8]

I praise You, Lord, for providing *all* the means for our healing, including the medical profession. But let me not be like King Asa, who even in his disease did not seek the Lord, but the physicians.[9]

Thank You for teaching me, Lord, how to fight with Your Word when the enemy comes to steal my health.

Jesus, You took my infirmities and carried away all my diseases,[10] and You send Your Word to heal me and deliver me from all destruction.[11] Lord, I will not forget any of Your benefits, for You not only pardon all my sins, but promise to heal all my diseases.[12]

I see that when I am assaulted by a physical problem, I can either let the symptoms cause me to doubt Your Word, or I can fight with the spiritual weapons You have provided: the sword of the Spirit, the blood of Jesus, the name of Jesus, praise and worship, etc. In fact, You have already won the battle for me, so I just stand in that victory. Having done all, I will stand![13]

Scripture Guide

My son, give attention to my words;
Incline your ear to my sayings.
Do not let them depart from your sight;
Keep them in the midst of your heart.
For they are life to those who find them,
And health [or medicine] to all their whole body.

Proverbs 4:20–22

Submit therefore to God.
Resist the devil and he will flee from you.

James 4:7

Meditation Response

What are ten things that I can praise the Lord for today? In what painful areas in my life do I need victory? Am I willing to thank God for these painful areas today, trusting that He will lead me to victory?

Doxology of Intimacy

O Lover of my soul, You have opened the windows of heaven since the first morning I came apart to seek Your face in prayer. It seems almost too good to be true, yet it *is* true and You have given it as a gift. The real reward, O Lord, is not victory over sin through Your overcoming power, but You.

I am experiencing a knowledge of You that I have not ever known was possible. Lord, I am so new! To what shall I attribute the change in my life except Your covenant faithfulness? You are answering all the prayers of my heart that I have prayed through years of bondage, defeat, emotional weakness, frustration, anxiety, even at times despair. O God, You work it all to the good. You have purposed good in Your heart for me all along.

You never left me through any of my rebellion. Who is a God like You who pardons iniquity and passes over the rebellious acts of a remnant of Your possession? You did not retain Your anger forever, for You delight in loving-kindness and unchanging love. You have again had compassion on me; You have trodden my iniquities underfoot; You have cast all my sins into the depths of the sea.[1]

Father, thank You for showing me my utter inability to keep a vow to You in my own strength. You will not let me see victory until I know it is Yours. Truly, it is Christ in me who is my hope of glory.[2]

In a way I have not ever experienced, You have put fear of You in my heart and granted me true godly sorrow and repentance.[3] Though conviction has been strong and heavy and I've been undone, I don't think I've ever tasted anything so sweet!

Yet, Lord, it has been a necessary process of being washed in Your Word, that Your Word is progressively working in me to produce faith—the faith You promised would come through Your Word. It is, in fact, Your divinely appointed way of coming into faith.[4]

I praise You that I am learning to fear any other way of doing something but Your appointed way. Glory to You, Father, that You are giving me the privilege of knowing Your way. The secret of the Lord is to those who fear Him. To them You make known Your covenant.[5]

I cherish, treasure, and hold to my breast Your covenant with me. You are my deliverer, Lord.[6] I've said that for years, but now *I am being delivered*. What a joy to experience in reality the truth of all I have said I believed, yet I praise You for leading me to *say* it even before it came to pass on a practical level.[7]

You have changed my heart. You are putting a hatred of sin in me that I have never known. You are causing me to see anything that keeps me from You as a viper! And all You promised is true, yea and amen![8] How much more precious are Your presence, Your Word, and Your will than any earthly thing or pleasure.[9] And what sweet rest! Your yoke really is easy and Your burden is light.[10]

Being with You, coming apart to behold Your beauty, has become my heart's greatest desire.[11] Your Word is satisfying the hunger and thirst You are producing in me for Your righteousness.[12]

Thank You for Your promise that in righteousness I will be established.[13] O Lord, increase Your grace in my life. Multiply it in the knowledge of Jesus[14]—though I hardly know how to contain it now. But don't let me contain it!

Spill out the overflow to all those around me. Let them taste, too, of Your goodness, mercy, faithfulness, and repentance. How different is Your repentance from worldly sorrow.[15]

And now, Father, though I care not how or when fruit is borne in and from my life, I rest in the truth and power of Your promise that "he who abides in Me, and I in him, he bears much fruit."[16] That fruit is an undeniable result of abiding in You.

Thank You for setting me free from striving. Jesus, I trust Your way. You are my faithful Shepherd forever.[17] How I love You. Though I know Your love surpasses knowledge,[18] I feel I am beginning for the first time to love the Lord my God with all my heart, soul, mind, and strength.[19] Perfect me in Your Love, O Lord, My faithful High Priest.

Scripture Guide

These verses, spoken thousands of years ago by the prophet Micah, have become precious to me, for I feel they are a powerful summary of what God has done in my life:

But as for me, I will watch expectantly for the Lord; I will wait for the God of my salvation. My God will hear me. Do not rejoice over me, O my enemy. Though I fall, I will rise; though I dwell in darkness, the Lord is a light for me. I will bear the indignation of the Lord because I have sinned against Him, until He pleads my case and executes justice for me. He will bring me out to the light, and I will see His righteousness [in the Amplified Bible, *RIGHTEOUS DELIVERANCE*]. Then my enemy will see, and shame will cover her who said to me, "Where is the Lord your God?"

Micah 7:7–10

Meditation Response

After using this handbook for my personal devotions, what is my own "doxology of intimacy" with my Lord?

Epilogue

I want to encourage those of you who have made this journey with me to expect God to reward you for diligently seeking Him.[1] He promises in His Word to do just that and He cannot lie.[2]

Have you realized as you have traveled with me that we've been preparing a highway for the King?[3]

I pray that the valleys of discouragement and fear in your life have been lifted up, since Jesus is our glory and the lifter of our heads;[4] that any crooked places of unbelief or deceitfulness have been made straight, knowing He leads us in paths of righteousness for His name's sake;[5] that mountains of pride or self-sufficiency have been brought low as you have come to know more deeply the One who is meek and lowly of heart—that you've found rest for your soul.[6]

It is significant that the prophet Joel speaks of a mighty outpouring of the Holy Spirit that will come only after the hearts of the people have been prepared through calling a solemn assembly, consecrating a fast, rending their hearts and not their garments, and returning to God with all their hearts, with fasting, weeping, and mourning. In fact, Joel called all God's people to an all-night prayer meeting of brokenness and humility.[7]

As you have broken up your fallow ground, you have chosen that good part that Mary found and Jesus said would not be taken from her.[8] I pray you will keep your lamp trimmed with the oil of His Spirit as did the five wise virgins,[9] through spending intimate time with the Bridegroom in the prayer closet, sitting at His feet, poring over His Word and worshiping Him; and that you have come to require by vital necessity His presence.

You've probably met some strong enemies head-on along this journey, but I trust you've learned how much greater the One in us truly is.[10] He is our mighty Warrior, the Lion of the tribe of Judah[11] who always causes us to triumph over every foe.[12]

Though the enemy of our souls pressure us constantly to back off from God's Word, come under our circumstances, and wallow in despair, praise God that we are learning to rise up, call Satan's bluff, and pressure *him* for a change!

He will not let us go free from any bondage unless we make him let us go in Jesus' name. He hates it when we get a revelation of our authority as believers. Yet constant spiritual pressure on the enemy *will* cause him to release us if we don't give up before we see the victory.

As we come into a deeper revelation of all that was accomplished at Calvary and lean hard on our blood covenant with the living God through His Son, we will begin to see all the "Goliaths" in our lives as merely uncircumcised Philistines with no covenant whatever with our God. The bigger the "giants," the more glory to God as they topple one by one![13]

For this purpose Jesus gave Himself for us—that He might redeem us from every lawless deed and purify for Himself a people for His own possession.[14] He loves us too much to leave us slaves of any sin. If the Son shall make us free, we shall be free indeed.[15]

As we return to Jesus as our first love, the glory of the Lord shall be revealed and all mankind shall see it together; for the mouth of the Lord has spoken it.[16]

Let us go, then, to the highways and byways and invite others to travel along this holy highway with us,[17] knowing that their joyful destination also will be the glory of our King, Jesus!

Yes, the glory of the Lord *is* our exceeding great reward.[18]

Notes

I. A Journey Begun

The Missing Ingredient

1. 1 Peter 1:8
2. Revelation 2:4
3. Luke 7:47
4. John 10:10b
5. Ephesians 1:19a
6. John 1:12
7. 1 John 5:5
8. Revelation 2:5
9. Numbers 11:1–6; 14
10. Revelation 3:18c
11. Psalm 27:4b; 2 Chronicles 20:21
12. Isaiah 50:4–5
13. John 10:4
14. Deuteronomy 30:6
15. Hebrews 4:12
16. 1 John 5:3
17. Revelation 2:4–5
18. Mark 1:4–5, 15
19. Ephesians 3:20
20. Revelation 2:4–5
21. Hebrews 4:9–10
22. Ephesians 5:27
23. Matthew 25:4
24. Jeremiah 4:3; Hosea 10:12

My Covenant with the Lord

1. Philippians 2:13
2. Psalm 121:5, 7
3. Galatians 6:8
4. Romans 8:6
5. Luke 22:31–32

II. Sins of Omission

Lack of Love for God

1. Matthew 22:36–38
2. Exodus 20:3
3. Proverbs 4:23
4. Isaiah 26:3
5. 2 Corinthians 7:10
6. 1 John 4:10
7. Romans 5:5
8. Deuteronomy 6:5
9. Matthew 22:36–38
10. John 15:5b
11. Philippians 4:13
12. Philippians 4:19
13. 1 John 4:8
14. Romans 4:20–21
15. Matthew 7:7
16. Song of Solomon 5:16

Neglect of the Bible

1. Psalm 119:89
2. 2 Timothy 3:16
3. Romans 12:2
4. Deuteronomy 8:3
5. Isaiah 40:8
6. 1 John 1:9
7. Philippians 2:13
8. Psalm 119:11
9. Isaiah 50:4b

Unbelief

1   Romans 1:18b
2   2 Corinthians 10:5
3   Romans 1:21
4   Romans 12:2
5   Luke 18:8
6   Hebrews 11:6
7   Romans 10:17
8   Isaiah 55:11
9   Mark 9:24
10 James 1:6
11 Hebrews 4:2
12 Habakkuk 2:4
13 Hebrews 10:39
14 2 Timothy 3:5
15 Galatians 2:20b

Neglect of Prayer

1   Zechariah 12:10
2   Isaiah 58:12b
3   2 Corinthians 10:4
4   1 Samuel 12:23
5   2 Corinthians 9:8
6   Jude 20

Neglect of Grace

1   2 Corinthians 9:8
2   Ephesians 2:10
3   2 Corinthians 12:7
4   Romans 5:17
5   Lamentations 3:22–23

Indifference to Christian Duties

1   Hebrews 10:25
2   John 15:5b
3   Philippians 2:13
4   James 1:22
5   Luke 8:15

Unconcern for the Souls of Family and Friends

1   John 15:16
2   Romans 5:5

Unconcern for Lost Souls in the World

1   Matthew 6:19
2   Romans 9:2–3
3   1 John 2:15

Failure to Guard Against Discouragement

1   Luke 8:15
2   Ecclesiastes 5:5
3   Psalm 51:11
4   Hebrews 13:5b
5   1 John 1:9
6   Romans 6:1–4, 14
7   Romans 8:2
8   Matthew 26:41
9   1 Peter 5:8
10 John 10:10
11 Luke 18:1 *ff.*
12 Genesis 32:26

Failure to Trust God with My Children

1   James 1:22
2   1 John 5:14–15
3   Psalm 119:34
4   Hebrews 11:6
5   Isaiah 55:6
6   Matthew 6:10
7   John 17:15
8   Psalm 19:12–13
9   Matthew 12:29; 18:18
10 Luke 10:19
11 2 Timothy 1:12b
12 Isaiah 54:13

13 Exodus 12: 1
   Corinthians 5:7
14 2 Peter 3:9b
15 2 Timothy 2:20–21
16 Revelation 19:13; Colossians 1:18, Matthew 6:33
17 2 Timothy 2:22; Colossians 3:5; 1 John 2:15–17; James 4:4
18 Proverbs 9:10
19 1 John 5:14
20 Hebrews 4:16
21 Isaiah 43:26

Neglect of Family Duties

1 1 Corinthians 7:4
2 2 Corinthians 9:8
3 1 Corinthians 13:1–8
4 James 3:14–18
5 1 Corinthians 4:2
6 Luke 16:1–2

Neglect of Social Responsibilities

1 Amos 5:24
2 Matthew 5:13–14
3 Luke 19:13
4 Psalm 119:37
5 Habakkuk 3:2

Failure to Guard Against Sinful Behavior

1 Galatians 6:8
2 1 Peter 3:10
3 Revelation 3:18
4 Ephesians 5:26, 1 John 1:7
5 Hebrews 1:9
6 Psalm 86:11b
7 Proverbs 8:13
8 Genesis 50:20

9 John 8:44c
10 1 Peter 3:4
11 James 1:19
12 John 7:38
13 Ephesians 4:29
14 Ezekiel 36:26; Jeremiah 31:33
15 Romans 6:11
16 Romans 6:13
17 Hebrews 1:9
18 1 John 5:14–15
19 Romans 4:17
20 Romans 6:4
21 Romans 6:11

Reluctance to Give Correction

1 Matthew 7:3
2 John 7:24
3 Ephesians 4:15
4 2 Timothy 4:2

Neglect of Self-Denial

1 Galatians 5:22–24
2 Romans 8:37
3 Psalm 119:133
4 Luke 9:23
5 Ephesians 3:20
6 James 4:4
7 Colossians 3:5–6
8 Philippians 4:4–5
9 1 Peter 2:20–23
10 2 Timothy 3:12
11 1 Corinthians 1:18
12 Galatians 5:6
13 Romans 10:17, Revelation 19:13; John 1:14
14 Philippians 3:10
15 Philippians 3:8

Lack of the Fear of God

1 Romans 2:4b

III. Sins of Commission

Ingratitude

1 Corinthians 10:11
2 Deuteronomy 8:2–3
3 Hebrews 3:19
4 John 16:8
5 Matthew 3:8
6 James 2:13
7 Psalm 103:10
8 Isaiah 44:22a
9 Jeremiah 31:34c;
   Hebrews 8:12; 10:17
10 Hebrews 11:6

The "God" of Sleep

1 2 Corinthians 7:10
2 Romans 8:37

Worldliness

1 James 1:27
2 Galatians 5:19–21
3 Psalm 101:3
4 1 John 2:15–16
5 James 4:4
6 Colossians 3:1–2
7 Matthew 6:19–21
8 Hebrews 11:24–26

Pride

1 Proverbs 6:17
2 Psalm 51:17
3 James 4:6
4 Isaiah 64:8
5 Isaiah 45:9
6 2 Timothy 2:20
7 2 Timothy 2:21

Envy

1 Romans 8:29
2 Matthew 16:24

Criticalness

1 Titus 2:4; Ephesians
   5:22–24, 33b
2 Proverbs 31:11–12
3 James 1:19
4 Romans 15:7
5 Colossians 3:13
6 Ephesians 4:29
7 Matthew 21:12; 1 Peter
   2:5
8 Galatians 4:19
9 John 17:21
10 James 4:11; Galatians
   5:15
11 Zechariah 4:6

Lying

1 Revelation 21:8; 1 Corinthians 6:9–10
2 Jeremiah 17:9

Cheating

1 James 4:11

Hypocrisy

1 2 Corinthians 7:10
2 Proverbs 4:23
3 Mark 9:24

Robbing God

1 Mark 7:11
2 Matthew 23:23
3 Matthew 21:21

Bad Temper

1 Hebrews 12:1
2 Deuteronomy 30:19–20
3 Matthew 26:41

IV. On to Higher Ground

A New Beginning

1 Genesis 3:4–5
2 1 Corinthians 10:13
3 Titus 2:11–12

Prayer of Agreement

1 Galatians 5:23
2 Matthew 26:41
3 2 Corinthians 3:18

The Law of Love

1 1 Corinthians 13:1–3
2 Matthew 22:36–40
3 Deuteronomy 30:11, 14
4 1 John 4:7–8, 12
5 1 John 2:29; 4:8; 5:4

The Power of My Words

1 Proverbs 18:21
2 Matthew 12:34b
3 Hosea 5:15a
4 Philemon 6
5 Psalm 119:11; 19:12–13
6 Isaiah 55:11
7 Hebrews 3:1
8 Hebrews 13:15
9 Matthew 12:37
10 Ephesians 6:16
11 Zechariah 4:6–7; Matthew 17:20; 21:21; see also Luke 17:6; Mark 11:22–24
12 Matthew 21:22
13 Mark 11:23
14 Mark 11:25–26
15 James 3:6
16 Psalm 50:23
17 Psalm 119:89

The Power of a Biblical Fast

1 Luke 18:9–14
2 Matthew 6:16
3 Matthew 9:15
4 Matthew 6:17–18
5 Matthew 17:21; Mark 9:29
6 Matthew 17:14–21

A Time for War

1 1 Peter 5:8
2 Ephesians 6:13 *ff.*
3 Hosea 4:6a
4 Luke 4:18
5 Romans 6:6
6 Revelation 12:10
7 Hebrews 4:12
8 John 14:6
9 1 Thessalonians 5:8
10 2 Corinthians 5:21
11 Isaiah 52:7
12 2 Corinthians 10:5
13 Philippians 4:8
14 1 Thessalonians 5:8
15 Hebrews 11:1
16 Romans 15:13
17 See Matthew 4:1–11
18 Ephesians 6:18
19 Revelation 12:11
20 Acts 16:25–26
21 Philippians 2:9
22 Song of Solomon 1:3
23 Genesis 22:14
24 Exodus 17:15
25 Judges 6:22–24
26 Exodus 15:26
27 Exodus 31:13
28 Psalm 23:1
29 Jeremiah 23:6
30 Ezekiel 48:35

Rejecting Satan's Lies

1 John 8:44
2 John 8:31–32
3 John 10:10b
4 Romans 8:28; Philippians 4:19; 2 Corinthians 9:10
5 Romans 5:5b.
6 Proverbs 11:21b
7 Isaiah 44:3b
8 1 Peter 2:24
9 Mark 11:24

Wholeness through God's Word

1 1 Corinthians 10:13
2 Hebrews 13:8
3 Acts 10:38
4 1 John 3:8b
5 Colossians 2:15
6 3 John 2
7 Romans 12:2
8 Isaiah 53:5d; 1 Peter 2:24
9 2 Chronicles 16:12
10 Isaiah 53:4; Matthew 8:17
11 Psalm 107:20
12 Psalm 103:3
13 Ephesians 6:13

Doxology of Intimacy

1 Micah 7:18–19
2 Colossians 1:27
3 2 Corinthians 7:10
4 Romans 10:17
5 Psalm 25:14

6 Psalm 18:2
7 Psalm 107:2; Romans 4:17–18
8 2 Corinthians 1:20
9 Psalm 16:11
10 Matthew 11:30
11 Psalm 27:4
12 Matthew 5:6
13 Isaiah 54:14
14 2 Peter 1:2
15 2 Corinthians 7:10
16 John 15:5
17 Psalm 23:1
18 Ephesians 3:19
19 Deuteronomy 6:5

Epilogue

1 Hebrews 11:6
2 Titus 1:2
3 Isaiah 40:3–4
4 Psalm 3:3
5 Psalm 23:3
6 Matthew 11:29
7 Joel 1:13–14; 2:12–17, 28
8 Luke 10:42
9 Matthew 25:1–13
10 1 John 4:4
11 Revelation 5:5
12 2 Corinthians 2:14
13 1 Samuel 17:32–51
14 Titus 2:14
15 John 8:36
16 Isaiah 40:5
17 Matthew 22:10
18 Isaiah 58:8c; Genesis 15:16